MUSIC THEORY

*the text of this book is printed
on 100% recycled paper*

About the Author

George Thaddeus Jones is a composer and teacher of music theory living in Washington, D.C. He received his undergraduate training at the University of North Carolina and his master's and doctor's degrees in composition from the Eastman School of Music, University of Rochester. He has received numerous awards and grants, among them a Fulbright research grant to study in Italy, a Benjamin Commission, a grant for a Cooperative Research Project from HEW, and a Cultural Exchange grant for research in Romania. Since 1950 he has taught composition and theory at The Catholic University of America, and since 1961 has been Professor of Music.

MUSIC THEORY

by

George Thaddeus Jones

BARNES & NOBLE BOOKS

A DIVISION OF HARPER & ROW, PUBLISHERS

New York, Hagerstown, San Francisco, London

First BARNES & NOBLE BOOKS edition published 1974
LIBRARY OF CONGRESS CATALOG CARD NUMBER: 72–7762
ISBN: 0-06-460137-4

78 79 80   12 11 10 9 8 7

For Mary, Gwen, and Carol

Contents

Preface   xv
Introduction   xvii

I. Notation, Terminology, and Basic Theory

1. Elementary Acoustics and the Properties of Sound   3

2. Music Notation   11
    THE TWO AXES: TIME AND PITCH   11
    RHYTHM: NOTE VALUES AND RESTS   11
    DOTS AND TIES   13
    METER, BEAT, AND TEMPO   14
    TIME SIGNATURES: SIMPLE AND COMPOUND TIME   17
    ARTIFICIAL DIVISION AND SYNCOPATION   19
    PITCH: STAFF, CLEF, AND LEDGER LINES   20
    LETTER NAMES, SOLFEGE SYLLABLES, AND ACCIDENTALS   22
    OCTAVE DESIGNATIONS   25
    MANUSCRIPT WRITING AND ADDITIONAL SYMBOLS   26

3. Intervals and Scales   31
    BASIC INTERVALS: HALF STEPS AND WHOLE STEPS   31
    SCALES: CHROMATIC, MAJOR, AND MINOR   32
    KEY SIGNATURES AND CIRCLE OF FIFTHS   34
    INTERVALS   36
    RELATIVE, PARALLEL, AND CLOSELY RELATED KEYS   40
    MEDIEVAL CHURCH MODES   42
    WHOLE-TONE SCALES   43
    PENTATONIC SCALES   44
    OTHER SCALES   44
    TUNING SYSTEMS AND TEMPERAMENT   45

4. Chords   49

CONSONANCE AND DISSONANCE   49
TRIADS: ROOT POSITION AND INVERSIONS   52
SEVENTH CHORDS AND LARGER STRUCTURES IN
    SUPERIMPOSED THIRDS   53
OTHER CHORD STRUCTURES   55

5. Symbolization   59

BASIC SYMBOLS AND DEFINITIONS   59
NAMES OF SCALE DEGREES AND CHORDS   60
FIGURED BASS   61
ROMAN NUMERAL CHORD SYMBOLS: FUNCTIONAL
    HARMONY   63
CHORD SYMBOLS IN JAZZ AND POPULAR MUSIC   69

6. Expression Marks and Foreign-Language Terms   73

TEMPO   73
DYNAMICS   74
STYLE   75
PHRASING AND ARTICULATION   76
ABBREVIATIONS   78
FOREIGN NAMES FOR SCALE DEGREES AND KEYS   80

    II. Tonal Harmony

7. Tonality and Key Feeling   85

TONALITY   85
KEY FEELING   91
MODULATION, SECONDARY DOMINANTS, AND
    ALTERED CHORDS   94
ASSIGNMENTS   100

8. Melody Writing   101

SMALL STROPHIC FORMS   102
    A. MOTIVE   102
    B. PHRASE-MEMBER   102
    C. PHRASE   102
    D. PERIOD   102
    E. DOUBLE PERIOD   102
    F. PHRASE-GROUP   102

SYMMETRY AND BALANCE   104
METRIC STRUCTURE   104
MELODIC CADENCES   106
THE FINAL CADENCE   106
INTERIOR CADENCES   108
EXTENSIONS AND IRREGULARITIES   110
ASSIGNMENTS   111

9. Four-Part Vocal Texture (SATB)   113
VOICE RANGES   114
DOUBLING   114
SPACING, DISTANCE, MOTION, AND
      CROSSING OF PARTS   116
CHORD INVERSIONS   117
PROHIBITIONS IN FOUR-PART WRITING   118
ASSIGNMENTS   122

10. Chord Connection   123
PRINCIPLES OF PART WRITING—TRIADS IN
      ROOT POSITION   124
      A. REPEATED TRIADS   125
      B. TRIADS A FIFTH APART   126
      C. TRIADS A SECOND APART   127
      D. TRIADS A THIRD APART   129
TRIADS IN FIRST INVERSION   131
TRIADS IN SECOND INVERSION   132
EXERCISES   135

11. Chord Choice   141
HARMONIC CADENCES   143
SELECTING THE CHORDS   144
MELODIC CADENCES   150
THE BASS LINE   151
THE INNER PARTS   156
EXERCISES   157

12. Harmonizing a Melody   159
ANALYSIS OF THE MELODY   159
HARMONIZING AN UNFIGURED BASS   161
EXERCISES   163

III. *Elaboration*

13. Nonharmonic Tones (Melodic Elaboration)   169
DEFINITIONS   171
PASSING TONE   172
NEIGHBORING TONE   176
SUSPENSION AND ANTICIPATION   179
APPOGGIATURA AND ESCAPE TONE   186
PEDAL, FREE TONE, COMBINATIONS   190
HARMONIZATIONS USING NONHARMONIC TONES   195
EXERCISES   198

14. Seventh and Ninth Chords (Harmonic
Elaboration)   199
V^7 AND VII^7 201
II^7 AND IV^7 208
DISSONANT CHORDS ON OTHER FUNCTIONS:
    VI, I, AND III   213
NINTH CHORDS   215
ELEVENTH AND THIRTEENTH CHORDS   220
EXERCISES   226

15. Altered Chords and Chromaticism
(Tonal Elaboration)   229
THE PRINCIPLE OF MELODIC ALTERATION   230
RAISED TONES: SECONDARY DOMINANTS,
    AUGMENTED TRIADS   231
LOWERED TONES: LOWERED SIXTH DEGREE,
    NEAPOLITAN CHORD   234
RAISED AND LOWERED TONES: AUGMENTED SIXTH
    CHORDS, THE ALTERED DOMINANT CHORD,
    OTHER FUNCTIONS   237
HARMONIC ALTERATION   243
REMOTE MODULATION   249
BY CHANGE-OF-MODE (MAJOR, MINOR)   249
CHAIN MODULATION   251
THE CHROMATIC THIRD-RELATION   258
THE TWELVE-TONE SCALE   258

16. Solving Figured Bass   263
MODELS FOR PRACTICE   264
EXERCISES   268

17. Analysis and Score Reading   271

KEYBOARD STYLE   271

SOLO INSTRUMENT (OR VOICE) WITH
ACCOMPANIMENT   277

TRIOS, QUARTETS, AND SMALL ENSEMBLES   280

THE FULL ORCHESTRAL SCORE   281

THE ANALYSIS OF AN EXTENDED WORK   286

Appendix 1

FOREIGN-LANGUAGE NAMES FOR ORCHESTRAL
INSTRUMENTS   291

Appendix 2

RANGE AND TRANSPOSITION OF ORCHESTRAL
INSTRUMENTS   294

Appendix 3

DIAGRAMS OF HOMOPHONIC FORMS   298

Appendix 4

BACH CHORALES FOR ANALYSIS   300

Bibliography   305

Index   307

Preface

A basic music theory course should be concerned with the information and skills one needs to read and understand music. This outline is designed primarily for the college-age music student, but it may also be used by the younger student and by the non-professional adult, since it assumes no prerequisites and encompasses all of the fundamental concepts of tonal music.

The material covered is essentially that which is contained in music theory or harmony courses on the college level, that is, notation, terminology, the reading and writing skills of harmony, analysis, and score reading. This assumes, as do most music school curricula, that the more specialized skills of counterpoint, orchestration, and form will be treated in depth in individual courses. However, certain basic knowledge that is needed for the reading and analysis of scores—for example, clefs and instrumental transposition—is treated either in the body of the text or in an appendix that follows.

The table of contents sets forth the organization of the material covered, so that, as with any dictionary or encyclopedia, one may look up an individual concept and find a relatively complete explanation or definition of it. At the end of the volume will be found the appendixes, an index, and a bibliography of books for further study.

Introduction

In music, as in many other fields, theory follows practice. The conventions that we call music theory have been derived, over a long period of time, from the analysis of the works and practices of the master composers.

The aim of beginning theory is to acquaint the student with the general concepts and terminology that will be most useful to him in playing and analyzing the music in today's repertory. Most performers and listeners will be primarily concerned with the music of the last three hundred years—music from the baroque, classic, romantic, and contemporary eras.

Within the past three centuries there can be found seemingly contradictory fashions; for example, the parallelism found in French impressionism is not found in the classic period, but these details can be explained after the student acquires the rudiments of tonal language.

Details and fashions change with different periods in music history, but this fact should not be used as an excuse to make the study of music theory a study of musical style. The style of a particular period is more properly a musicological undertaking and something the student will concern himself with later.

Music theory encompasses both information and skills, that is, information that must be memorized and basic skills that must be acquired. The acquisition of the basic material is best accomplished through drill, repetition, and a reasonable volume of work.

Part I
Notation, Terminology, and
Basic Theory

Chapter 1

Elementary Acoustics
and the Properties of Sound

The sensation of sound is produced when *vibrations* transmitted through the air strike the eardrum. Irregular and complex vibrations are usually classified as *noise,* while regular vibrations produce *tones* of a discernible *pitch.*

A vibration is produced by the oscillation of some elastic material, such as a stretched string. This is transmitted by the molecules in the air forming areas of compression and rarefaction. One vibration in the air consists of one cycle or wave of high- and low-pressure areas.

The number of these vibrations per second is called the *frequency* of the sound wave; the greater the frequency, the higher the pitch. The strength or *amplitude* of the vibration controls the *volume* or intensity of the sound; the greater the amplitude the louder the sound.

Tones have certain properties and characteristics for which we have terms:

Pitch: the relative sense of "high" or "low"
Duration: the length of the sound or rhythm
Intensity: the volume or degree of loudness
Timbre: the distinctive quality of the sound.

These are the principal properties that interest the musician, although some other aspects will have significance in the area of performance: for example, how the tone is attacked or released, how one tone is connected with another, and how a combination of tones produces a sense of density or texture.

Musical instruments are mechanisms that produce, resonate,

3

amplify, and otherwise control vibrations. Sometimes they are categorized according to the principal material out of which they are constructed, as, for example, brass or woodwind instruments. However, from an acoustical point of view, it is better to discuss the common musical instruments under the headings of vibrating strings, vibrating air columns, and vibrating bars, plates, or membranes.

VIBRATING STRINGS

String instruments can be subdivided according to how the string is set in motion. Bowed instruments include the violin, viola, cello, bass, and the obsolete family of viols; plucked instruments include the harp, harpsichord, guitar, lute, mandolin, and banjo; struck string instruments are the piano, clavichord, and cimbalon. Whatever the method of setting the string in vibration, it reacts acoustically in substantially the same way for all of these instruments.

Given a string of elastic material secured at both ends:

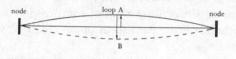

Figure 1

If it is moved out of its position of rest to point *A* by being struck, plucked, or bowed, the elasticity of the string and its momentum will carry it to point *B*, a distance past the point of rest approximately equal to the original displacement (*A*). If it is then left free to vibrate, it will eventually be brought again to a state of rest by the friction of the medium, in this case air. The degree of displacement, which is the amplitude, determines the loudness of the sound. One entire cycle, from point of rest to *A*, then to *B*, and back to point of rest, is considered one vibration or wave; the ends of the string are the *nodes* of the wave, the center point is called the *loop*. While many things affect the pitch produced by a string—the material out of which it is made, its thickness, and its tension—its pitch is primarily determined by the string length.

The vibration of the entire length of the string as shown in figure 1 produces the *fundamental,* that is, the basic pitch we assign to this string length. However, being flexible the string vibrates also in parts of halves, thirds, quarters, and so on, and each of these segments produces a sound. These sounds are called *partials,* or *overtones.*

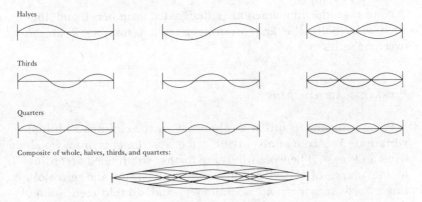

Figure 2

This composite sound accompanies the fundamental and is called the *overtone series.* Given a string of the correct length to produce C, the following series of pitches will result from the partial vibrations:

Figure 3

The pitches are shown in our "tempered scale" notation, and are only approximate; the space between the partials decreases proportionately as the series ascends. The series does not stop at the sixteenth partial, but this segment is, for practical purposes, all that we need be concerned with. The fundamental and the lower partials have greater intensity and are therefore easier to hear than some of the more remote overtones, but it would be an oversimplification to say that the series gradually diminishes in intensity as it ascends. In the *timbre,* or characteristic tone color, of some instruments certain of the upper partials are stronger than certain others, and it is due partly to this fact that we are able to distinguish one instrument from another—an oboe from a flute, for example.

Note that the fundamental is designated number 1 and that what is actually the first overtone is called number 2 in the overtone series.

Vibrating air columns

Wind instruments utilize a column of air to reinforce an initial vibration. We commonly divide wind instruments into wood-wind and brass. The woodwinds are further subdivided according to the source of the vibration: edge tone (flute and piccolo), single reed (clarinet and saxophone), and double reed (oboe, English horn, and bassoon); the source of the vibration for all brass instruments (trumpet, horn, trombone, and tuba) is the performer's lips, which vibrate inside a cup mouthpiece.

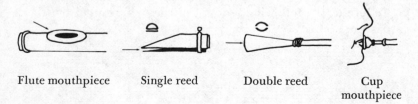

Flute mouthpiece   Single reed   Double reed   Cup mouthpiece

Figure 4

In playing the flute the player directs an air column against the edge of the tubing (this is like blowing across the top of a bottle); the splitting of the air column on the edge of the tube sets up a vibration that is reinforced by the air column within the tube. For the reed instruments the player directs a column of air between a single reed and a mouthpiece, or between two reeds; the reed or reeds vibrate and the air column within the tube picks up the vibration. The brass player buzzes his lips inside a cup mouthpiece; the air column within the pipe vibrates in sympathy with this vibration. Thus all wind instruments utilize the air column within the tube to reinforce or resonate the initial vibration.

Like a vibrating string, the pitch of a vibrating air column is principally controlled by its length. Wind instruments have mechanisms for increasing or decreasing a basic length of pipe, which, in turn, controls the length of the air column within it. For woodwind instruments the maximum length of the tube is the entire length of the instrument from the mouthpiece to the bell; this is shortened by opening holes in the tube which have been covered by keys or the player's fingers. Brass instruments, on the other hand, start with a minimum length of pipe and increase this by using valves (for the trumpet, horn, and tuba) to add additional crooks of tubing, or by using a slide (in the case of the trombone). On all wind instruments more than one tone is possible from each given length of tubing; the tube may be overblown to produce one of the upper partials (usually the second or third) from the overtone series.

The behavior of a vibrating air column is somewhat like that of a vibrating string in that it vibrates in its entirety (the fundamental) and also in parts, producing the same overtone series that was given in figure 3. However, there are different types of pipe, which give different acoustical reactions. These types are used not only in the construction of the orchestral instruments we have just mentioned but also in the construction of the pipe organ.

The bore of a pipe may be either *cylindrical* or *conical,* or, as in the case of brass instruments, certain portions of the pipe are cylindrical while other parts—the mouthpipe and the bell branch —are conical.

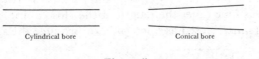

Cylindrical bore   Conical bore

Figure 5

These two types both react as *open pipes* acoustically, and the air column in such an open pipe will form both the node and the loop of the sound wave at the open end of the pipe.

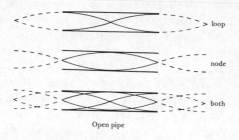

loop

node

both

Open pipe

Figure 6

This means that an open pipe will resonate both even- and odd-numbered partials in the overtone series, and can be overblown to produce the second overtone (the octave), the third overtone (the twelfth), or others. Also, one complete sound wave generated by an open pipe is twice the length of the pipe.

A different type of cylindrical bore has one closed end and is called a *closed pipe*.

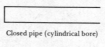

Closed pipe (cylindrical bore)

Figure 7

In the closed pipe only the loop of the sound wave will form at the open end.

Figure 8

This means two things acoustically: since a node will not form at the open end of the pipe, it will resonate only the odd-numbered overtones (1, 3, 5, and so on), and, since the complete sound wave is four times the length of the closed pipe, it requires only half as much closed as open pipe to produce the same pitch.

Figure 9

All orchestral instruments react as open pipes—and therefore overblow at the octave—except the clarinet family; the clarinets react acoustically as closed pipes and, since the second overtone is missing, overblow at the twelfth. The flute and oboe, for example, can produce the second overtone, an octave higher, from a given length of pipe, while the clarinet produces its second register using the third overtone, a twelfth higher.

Figure 10

Since it is a closed pipe, the clarinet can produce the same pitch as the flute or oboe with only half the length of pipe. This is why the clarinet has a lower register than the flute or oboe, although all three are approximately the same length.

There are certain other more complex characteristics of brass instruments—for example, they use a substantial number of the upper partials from the overtone series, and the tubing is partly cylindrical and partly conical—but these and other complications are better left to an orchestration course.

Vibrating bars, plates, and membranes

These are usually called *percussion instruments,* since various materials are struck with sticks, mallets, hammers, or beaters. They can conveniently be divided into two groups, one of instruments of definite pitch—timpani, xylophone, marimba, vibraphone, celesta, bells, and chimes—the other of instruments of indeterminate pitch—drums, cymbals, tambourine, and triangle.

The acoustics of membranes, plates, and bells cannot easily be graphically illustrated, since their vibration patterns are very complex. In fact, there is some mystery about the partial system of bells, and some disagreement about the actual pitch of the strike tone of a bell.

Instruments like the snare drum, cymbal, and gong have such complex and irregular vibrations that they produce no sensation of determinate pitch and are chiefly useful, in the orchestra, for rhythmic accentuation.

Before leaving the discussion of elementary acoustics, we must mention our tuning system. Western European civilization, unlike the cultures of the Far East and Africa, developed a musical system that is primarily harmonic and that derives from the natural overtone series given above. In order to make this harmonic system work without unnecessary complications, we have adopted a method based upon "octave equivalence." The entire range of useful musical sounds was divided up into segments that can be represented by the seven white and five black keys of the piano. This segment is called an *octave* (from the Latin *octo,* eight), since it is repeated beginning with each eighth white key on the piano keyboard; the white keys are designated by the first seven letters of the alphabet.

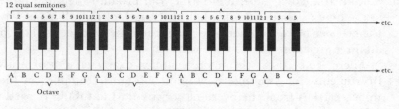

Figure 11

The space of an octave was then divided into twelve equal parts called *semitones* or *half steps.* This tuning system is convenient for purposes of chords, since each tone is equidistant from the next; however, the tones arrived at do not exactly agree with the pitches found in the natural overtone series. These tones were said to be *tempered,* that is, adjusted, and the tuning system was called *equal temperament,* since the twelve half steps are equal in size.

The music systems of some Eastern cultures are primarily concerned with melody, and so they have developed different tuning systems that contain smaller steps than the equal-tempered system; these steps are frequently called *third* or *quarter tones,* but these are only approximations.

Chapter 2

Music Notation

Music notation is the set of conventionally agreed-upon symbols by which the composer conveys his ideas, by way of the performer, to the listener.

THE TWO AXES: TIME AND PITCH

Music is essentially a temporal art. Unlike some other arts, traditional painting, for example, the performance (and perception) of a piece of music takes place during the passage of time. Music may be defined as organized pitches occurring in time. Notation must take into account the two dimensions, pitch and time. These are represented graphically on manuscript, or music-writing, paper by a set of conventional symbols using two axes: ┼ ; the passage of time is shown on the horizontal axis from left to right ⟶ , while the relative position of pitches is represented on the vertical axis: ↑ .

RHYTHM: NOTE VALUES AND RESTS

Rhythm is concerned with the duration or length in time of individual sounds. The relative lengths are indicated by a set of symbols called *notes;* silence is similarly shown by symbols called *rests.*

The names given the notes and rests refer to the fractional

11

parts of a measure of common time (see p. 19) .

Figure 12

Occasionally in older music a double whole note is found: ⬥️ ;
but this is rare today. Each note value or rest is equal to two
of the next smallest value or one half of the preceding value.

Figure 13

Eighth notes and smaller values may be written separately, with
individual flags, or they may be grouped together under *ligatures*
or *beams*. (See further details given below under manuscript
writing.)

Figure 14

Rests of corresponding values are always written separately,
that is, they are not connected by beams.

Figure 15

However, in practice several small rests seldom occur; their total value usually will be shown by a larger rest.

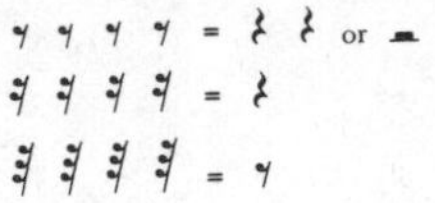

Figure 16

Dots and ties

A dot placed after a note or rest increases its value by one half.

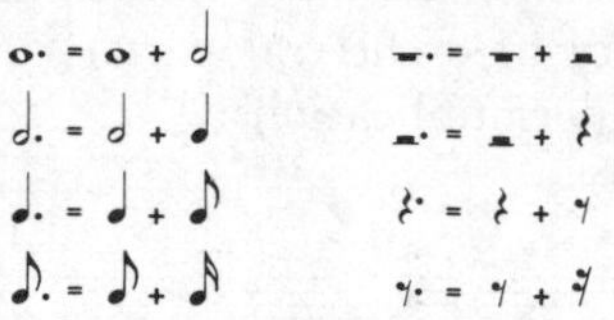

Figure 17

Each dotted note (or rest) is equal to two of the next smallest dotted notes or three of the next smallest notes without dots.

Although less frequently used, a second dot adds half the value of the first dot.

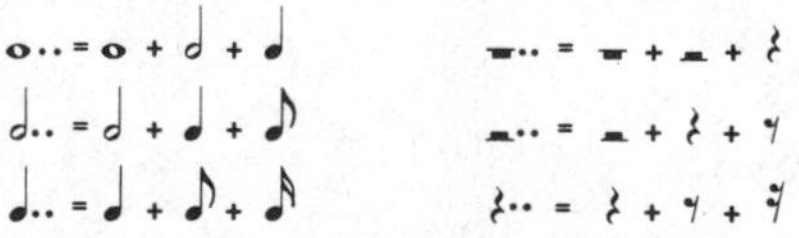

Figure 18

The length of notes may also be increased by the use of a *tie*. This is a curved line that connects notes of the same pitch, and these are performed as one note with the total value of the notes tied. Ties are not used to connect rests.

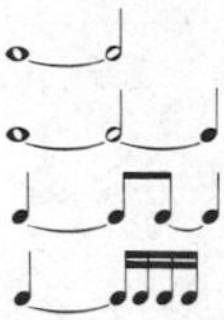

Figure 19

To indicate rests of a duration longer than a measure (as is sometimes necessary in orchestral parts), the following symbols may be found in older publications:

Figure 20

Today these symbols are seldom found; the preferred way now is to use a thick bar with the number of measures of rest written above it.

Figure 21

METER, BEAT, TEMPO

Meter is concerned with measure; rhythm refers to the length or duration of tones. These relative lengths, expressed by note symbols, must be measured accurately, one against another. In order to know the exact length of a tone, one must establish a regular pulsation, which is called the *beat,* against which lengths can be measured. The basic beat is what we express when we tap our foot, march, or dance to music. This background pulsation may be fast or slow, but it must be regular, so that it measures off equal increments of time. It is somewhat analogous to the increments of distance represented by the markings on a ruler or yardstick:

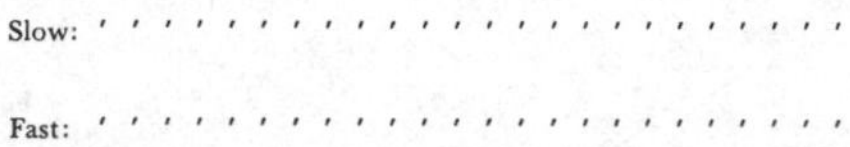

Slow: ′

Fast: ′

The speed at which we beat time is called the *tempo;* this is variable from very fast to very slow.

In order to better comprehend such a long succession of these regular beats, they are arranged in small groups called *measures,* and set off by *bar lines.* The first beat in each measure is accented; the remaining beats are unaccented. The number of beats within a measure is not arbitrary, but is chosen to best fit the rhythmic lengths and patterns of the music. Theoretically there might be from one to twelve beats within a measure, but in practice there are usually two, three, four, or six pulsations.

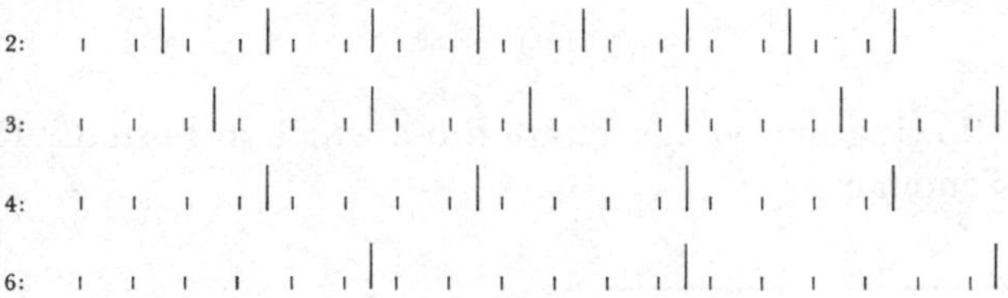

Figure 22

The recurrent groups of pulsations are called *meters:* for example, duple meter, triple meter, and quadruple meter.

The beats within the measures are counted and accented:

2: <u>one</u>, two | <u>one</u>, two |
3: <u>one</u>, two, three | <u>one</u>, two, three |
4: <u>one</u>, two, th<u>r</u>ee, four | <u>one</u>, two, th<u>r</u>ee, four |
6: <u>one</u>, two, three, f<u>ou</u>r, five, six |

These groupings may also be expressed by commonly agreed-upon conducting patterns.

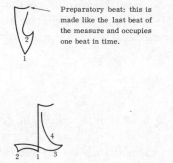

Conductor's beat: 2, 3, 4, and 6 beat pattern

Preparatory beat: this is made like the last beat of the measure and occupies one beat in time.

Figure 23

The tempo or actual speed is indicated by a metronomic notation, which shows the number of beats per minute , and by descriptive terms, usually in Italian, which are shown at the beginning of a piece.

Allegro   (♩ = 120)   Fast

Moderato   (♩ = 90)   Moderate

Adagio   (♩ = 60)   Slow

The following tempo figures are those which are usually found on a metronome:

(Slow) ⟶
40   50   60   72
  42, 44, 46, 48   52, 54, 56, 58,   63, 66, 69,   76,

    (Moderate) ⟶
    80   92   100   112
      84, 88,   96,   104, 108,   116

        (Fast) ⟶
        120   132   144   160   176   192   206
          126,   138,   152,   168,   184,   200,

Italian terms are frequently used to indicate approximate *tempi;* other Italian terms indicate a general style of performance, dynamics, or changes in tempi and dynamics. The most useful of these terms will be found, with their meanings, in Chapter 6.

TIME SIGNATURES: SIMPLE AND COMPOUND TIME

To represent the basic beat or pulsation we choose one of the note values given above. These may be represented by numbers.

Figure 24

The number of beats in each measure and the kind of note chosen to represent the beat are placed together as a fraction at the beginning of a composition. This is called the *time signature*. For example:

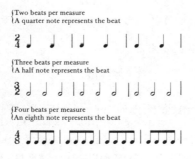

Figure 25

Time signatures represent *simple time* or *compound time,* depending upon how the basic beat is divided; in simple time the beat is divisible into *two* of the next smallest note values, in compound time it is divisible into *three* of the next smallest value.

Simple Time. The time signature may show any number from 1 to 12 as the upper figure; the lower figure will represent one of the basic note values (2, 4, 8, 16, and so on). The basic condition for simple time, however, is that *the beat is naturally divisible by two.* The common signatures are:

Simple duple: $\frac{2}{8}$ $\frac{2}{4}$ $\frac{2}{2}$ | $\frac{2}{4}$ = | ♩ ♩ | divisible | ♫ ♫ |

Simple triple: $\frac{3}{8}$ $\frac{3}{4}$ $\frac{3}{2}$ | $\frac{3}{4}$ = | ♩ ♩ ♩ | divisible | ♫ ♫ ♫ |

Simple quadruple: $\frac{4}{8}$ $\frac{4}{4}$ $\frac{4}{2}$ | $\frac{4}{4}$ = | ♩ ♩ ♩ ♩ | divisible | ♫ ♫ ♫ ♫ |

Figure 26

Unusual signatures will use 1, 5, or 7 as the upper figure, with one of the basic note values as the lower figure.

Compound Time. When *the basic beat is naturally divisible by three,* the music is in compound time. The upper figure will normally be 6, 9, or 12 and the lower figure will represent a basic note value (usually 2, 4, 8, or 16). In order to show the groupings by three, *dotted* note values represent the beat in compound time. The common signatures are:

Compound duple: $\frac{6}{8}$ $\frac{6}{4}$ $\frac{6}{2}$ | $\frac{6}{8}$ = | ♩. ♩. | divisible | ♪♪♪ ♪♪♪ |

Compound triple: $\frac{9}{8}$ $\frac{9}{4}$ $\frac{9}{2}$ | $\frac{9}{8}$ = | ♩. ♩. ♩. | divisible | ♪♪♪ ♪♪♪ ♪♪♪ |

Compound quadruple: $\frac{12}{8}$ $\frac{12}{4}$ $\frac{12}{2}$ | $\frac{12}{8}$ = | ♩. ♩. ♩. ♩. | divisible | ♪♪♪ ♪♪♪ ♪♪♪ ♪♪♪ |

Figure 27

There are some signatures that can be treated either as simple or as compound time; for example, $\frac{3}{8}$ is simple time when played three beats to the measure, but is compound if taken in one beat per measure. Some music will appear to be a combination or mixture of simple (2) and compound (3) groupings; for example, $\frac{5}{8}$ time, if played two beats to the measure, is two plus three or three plus two: | ♫ ♪♪♪ | or | ♪♪♪ ♫ | In this case, however, the beats are not of equal length, but the value of the eighth note remains the same.

In older music the same time signature was usually retained for a whole composition, or at least for a section of a piece. In contemporary music (and exceptionally in some older music) it is now common to find meter changes within a section or a phrase of music. When the meter changes it is necessary to know whether the length in time for each *beat* remains the same, or whether the *note value* remains the same.

Figure 28

Finally, two vestiges of an earlier notation system are found as time signatures today; these are: c , usually called *common time* and ¢ , usually called *alla breve.*

Figure 29

ARTIFICIAL DIVISION AND SYNCOPATION

The natural divisions in both simple and compound time may be altered to produce other note groupings. The general rule for the notation is to use the note value of the nearest natural division and to place the appropriate number above or below the group and under a slur or bracket. For example:

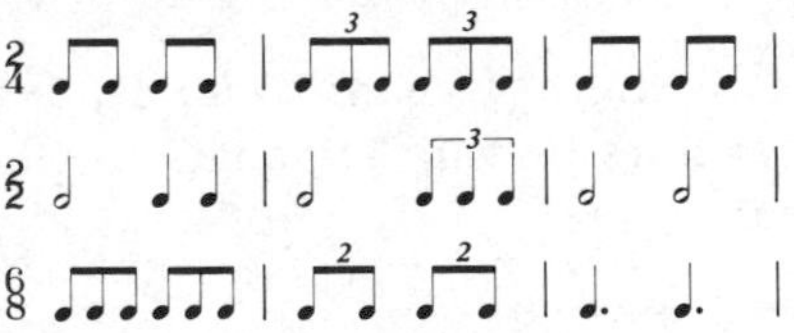

Figure 30

These are called *triplets, duplets,* and so on, and indicate that three notes are to be played in the time of two, or vice versa. Rarely, the duplet in compound time will be shown by a dot.

Figure 31

When short notes, ties, or rests are used to misplace the natural accents in music the effect is called *syncopation*. This is based upon an implied premise that long notes naturally occur on accented beats, or on the accented downbeat, while short notes naturally occur at unaccented places. For example:

Figure 32

PITCH: STAFF, CLEF, AND LEDGER LINES

The earliest attempts at pitch notation consisted of accent marks placed over the words of vocal music to remind the singer of the contour of an already-known melodic line. These staffless *neumes* only gave general direction to the line, and no precision in indicating pitch relations was possible until the staff was devised.

Staff. This was a scale (Italian, *scala:* ladder) consisting of parallel horizontal lines by which changes in pitch could be accurately measured.

Figure 33

Pitches were then indicated by placing the proper note value upon a line or space of this staff.

The so-called *great staff* of eleven lines encompasses approximately the entire range of men's voices. However, since most early vocal melodies were of limited compass, a smaller section (four or five lines) was sufficient for most music. The key to which four or five lines were being used was given by the placement of a letter (G, C, or F) on a line to be used as a point of reference.

Clef. These letters were called *clefs* (French, *clef:* key), and they have changed with time to become our modern forms of clefs.

Figure 34

The G clef is usually called the *treble* clef, the F clef is called the *bass* clef, and the C, or movable clef, survives in modern scores as the *alto* or *tenor* clef.

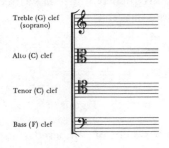

Treble (G) clef (soprano)

Alto (C) clef

Tenor (C) clef

Bass (F) clef

Figure 35

Older music, particularly vocal music, used the C clef in other positions, so that *middle C* occurred on each of the five lines; the common names of these clefs were:

Soprano   Mezzo-soprano   Alto   Tenor   Baritone

Figure 36

The G and F clefs also occurred on other lines, but these have no use today. In present-day vocal music, when the tenor part is written on a separate staff it is frequently notated in the G clef with an 8 below it to show that the part sounds an octave lower.

Figure 37

The compass of each staff may be increased by the use of additional short lines called *ledger lines*.

Figure 38

LETTER NAMES, SOLFEGE SYLLABLES, AND ACCIDENTALS

Pitches are indicated by placing the different note values given above on the proper line or space of the staff; the clefs indicate reference points. Frequently music is written on a pair of staves using the treble and bass clefs.

Figure 39

Today we use a system of tempered tuning that arranges the entire pitch spectrum into smaller segments called *octaves*. Each octave is divided into twelve equal parts called *half steps;* two half steps may be combined to produce a *whole step*. Since early vocal music used scales that generally had seven tones to each octave, we have a system of naming pitches with seven letters or *solfege* (singing) syllables.

A   B   C   D   E   F   G   (letters: German, English, American)
la si (ti) do re mi fa sol (solfege syllables: Italian, French)

The piano keyboard is a good graphic representation of the pitches found in the modern twelve-tone tempered scale system.

The space between two of the same letter names such as C to C is called an *octave,* that is, eight letter names. The white keys represent the arrangements of the early modal scales or our present seven-tone scales.

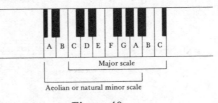

Figure 40

These seven-tone *scales* or *modes* are made up of different arrangements of whole and half steps and are called *diatonic* scales. The white keys on the piano are represented by the lines and spaces of the staff; the letter names for these are:

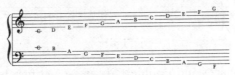

Figure 41

The notes in between these white keys are represented by the black keys on the piano. On the staff they are represented by raising one of the natural letter names one half step, with a symbol called a *sharp* (♯), or lowering it one half step, with a symbol called a *flat* (♭). A sign called a *natural* (♮) cancels a previous *accidental* (a raised or lowered letter name) and returns that note to its unaltered form. Accidentals are placed on the staff immediately *before* the note they affect, and they obtain for that note only for the duration of that particular measure, unless canceled. In speaking, we designate pitches by having the accidental *follow* the letter name, as: C♯ (C sharp) or D♭ (D flat) .

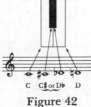

Figure 42

The scale that uses all of the half steps is called a *chromatic* scale; ascending scales are usually notated using sharps and descending scales using flats. The same sound or pitch written two different ways is said to be written *enharmonically*.

Chromatic scale:

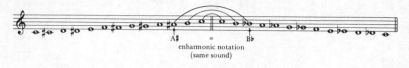

Figure 43

Occasionally a double sharp (**x**) or a double flat (bb) is used to indicate that a natural scale step has been raised or lowered two half steps, that is, one whole step.

Figure 44

Double sharps and double flats are sometimes found in music of the romantic period but today they are less used. Composers now try to notate music in the simplest way; the above examples could also be written:

Figure 45

An accidental placed in parenthesis (as in the first measure above) is usually intended as a *precautionary* accidental. An accidental is also used immediately across a bar line when this would clarify the composer's intention:

Figure 46

OCTAVE DESIGNATIONS

The range of pitches that can be heard by the human ear is quite large: roughly from 20 v.p.s. (vibrations per second) to 20,000 v.p.s. Music makes use of only a part of this possible range. For practical purposes the range of the piano is all that we need be concerned with; the total range of orchestral instruments, from the piccolo and violin to the contrabassoon and string bass, is slightly less than the piano. Our system of tuning is based upon octave equivalence, that is, the entire range of the modern keyboard is divided up into those smaller segments called octaves, which have the same pattern of steps and half steps and the same letter names. The white keys are assigned letter names and the black keys are designated by accidentals.

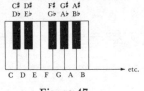

Figure 47

Since this pattern is represented throughout the entire range of the piano—a little more than seven octaves—it is necessary to have a system to designate particular octaves when these are not shown by staff notation.

Each octave is considered to begin with the letter C and extends up to the letter B; the next octave begins with C, and so on. The standard piano keyboard, however, begins with A and extends through seven octaves ending with C. The most commonly found system of identifying the various octaves is given below:

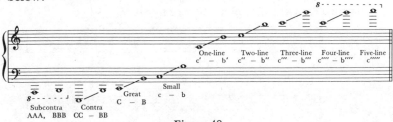

Figure 48

MANUSCRIPT WRITING AND ADDITIONAL SYMBOLS

There are some conventions of notation the student should know about and practice in manuscript writing.

On all notes smaller than a whole note, a stem is attached. Stems may extend up or down; ascending stems are placed to the right of the note head; descending stems are placed to the left. Flags are always to the right of the stems.

Figure 49

Measures are marked off by *bar lines.* At the end of a section a double bar line is used; at the end of a composition a thicker double bar may occur.

Figure 50

When two dots are used with the double bar, this means to repeat the section of music, either from the beginning or from the previous repeat sign.

Figure 51

D.C., an abbreviation for *da capo* (from the beginning), and D.S., an abbreviation for *dal segno* (from the sign), mean to repeat the music from the beginning or from this sign: ⅜ . When the sign ✦ is found, it usually means to go to the *coda* (Italian: tail) or the closing section of music.

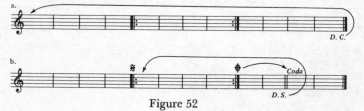

Figure 52

In making D.C. and D.S. returns, repeat marks within the section are ignored the second time.

Although all measures within a composition must be complete, it is not uncommon to find a piece that begins with a partial measure. The note (or notes) in a beginning partial measure is called an *anacrusis,* or "pick-up" note. It is customary to leave out of the final measure as much as the first partial bar contained, so that together they will add up to a complete measure.

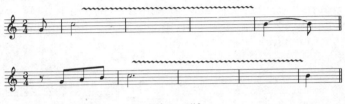

Figure 53

In counting measures, the first *complete* measure is counted as number one.

When a single part is written on one staff, the stems for the notes above the middle line all go down; the stems for the notes below the middle line all go up; the stems for the notes on the middle line may go either way.

Figure 54

When two parts share the same staff the stems for the upper part all go up, the stems for the lower part all go down, regardless of the position on the staff.

Figure 55

In vocal music that has a text, it was formerly the custom to write the small (eighth and sixteenth) notes with separate flags when these notes were sung to separate syllables; small notes sung to the same syllable were connected by beams or ligatures.

Figure 56. Schubert, "Auf dem Wasser zu singen"

Today, when rhythmic problems are often more difficult, many composers have adopted the policy of writing vocal music in the same way that instrumental music is written, that is, small notes are grouped together by beats so that the rhythm is more easily seen. Figure 57 shows the same fragment of the Schubert song in modern notation.

Figure 57

When a part is to be performed an octave higher or lower, this is indicated by 8 or 8ᵛᵃ with a dotted line extending above or below the part. This designation is often used to avoid writing ledger lines.

Figure 58

Later, there will be other conventions to be observed in writing chords and keyboard music and in indicating phrasing and articulation in instrumental parts.

Before continuing with additional material, let us review this chapter by showing some examples of how the individual concepts are combined in a piece of music.

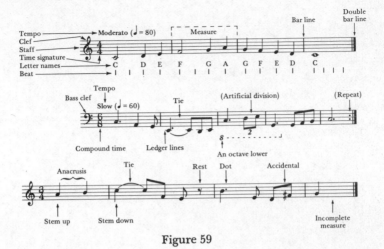

Figure 59

Chapter 3

Intervals and Scales

The distance between two tones is termed an *interval*. The smallest intervals are those of the half and whole step; these occur between adjacent letter names on the staff. On the white keys of the piano there is a half step between **E–F** and **B–C**; between all of the other letters there is a whole step.

Figure 60

The whole steps may be divided into half steps by the use of sharps or flats.

Figure 61

If the two tones comprising an interval occur together in time the interval is *harmonic;* if they occur one after the other the interval is *melodic.* In order to name intervals accurately, it is necessary to have two terms: one term is quantitative, representing the number of letters involved, including first and last; the other term is qualitative, requiring an additional modifying

31

term. For example, C to D is called a *major second* (a whole step), while E to F is a *minor second* (half step). While it is possible to describe larger intervals in terms of the number of half steps each contains, this is usually not done; larger intervals are described by relating them to the normal occurrences in the major scale.

SCALES: CHROMATIC, MAJOR, AND MINOR

From the earliest times, theorists have abstracted the tones used in a musical composition and placed them on a staff in order to study them. The tones are arranged in ascending stepwise order from the keynote; the patterns, or orders of tones, are called *scales*.

We will begin with the three most useful types of scale, chromatic, major, and minor, since these have the greatest use in eighteenth- and nineteenth-century music. Later we will discuss the medieval modal scales and some others, such as whole-tone, pentatonic, and symmetrical scales.

The nonselective scale, which contains all of the possible tones in equal temperament, is called the *chromatic* scale (or sometimes the *twelve-tone* or *duodecuple* scale.) Today it is usually notated in sharps ascending, and in flats descending.

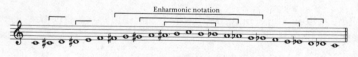

Figure 62

The most used selective scale for music of the last three hundred years is called the *major* scale.

Figure 63

In this scale, half steps occur between the third and fourth and between the seventh and eighth degrees; between all other degrees there is a whole step.

The next most useful scale, the *minor* scale, has three forms, that is, a basic pattern of whole and half steps and two variations of this pattern.

The *natural minor* scale was derived from the Aeolian mode (which is discussed below). In it, half steps occur between the second and third and between the fifth and sixth degrees.

Figure 64

In practical composition it was customary to raise the seventh degree of this scale to strengthen cadential points; this produced the *harmonic* form of the minor scale. In it, half steps occur between the second and third, the fifth and sixth, and the seventh and eighth steps. One and a half steps (*augmented second*) occur between the sixth and seventh degrees.

Figure 65

In order to avoid the awkward interval between the sixth and seventh degrees of this scale, another adjustment was often made, particularly in vocal music. The *melodic minor* scale raises both the sixth and seventh degrees in its ascending form; the descending form of the melodic minor scale reverts to the form of the natural minor. In it, half steps occur between the second and third and between the seventh and eighth degrees ascending, and it reverts to the natural minor scale descending.

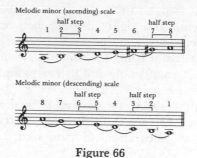

Figure 66

KEY SIGNATURES AND CIRCLE OF FIFTHS

The patterns for the major and natural minor scales must be constructed upon each of the possible twelve chromatic pitches. The student should do this taking each tone systematically as the first note. He must keep in mind the whole- and half-step arrangement of the unaltered (white-key) letter names and create the correct pattern for the scale using the necessary accidentals. Only one kind of accidental (that is, sharps or flats) should be used in any single major or natural minor scale. For example, if we begin to construct a major scale on A we need the following three sharps:

Figure 67

If we construct a natural minor scale on C we require three flats.

Figure 68

For the sake of convenience, these accidentals are collected and arranged at the beginning of a musical composition and are termed its *key signature*. This key signature applies until it is canceled by naturals or until another key signature displaces it. One major and one minor key will share the same signature.

These two keys are said to be *related,* or one is the *relative minor* or *relative major* of the other. By common agreement the pattern of the accidentals assembled in the key signatures always follows the designs given below. These signatures of the major and minor scales, with their respective keynotes, must be memorized, and the student should practice writing these on the staff.

Figure 69. Key signatures: major and relative minor

The student will notice that, beginning with the letter C, the sharp keys make an ascending progression in fifths, and the flat keys a descending progression in fifths (that is, every fifth letter name.) This is often described as the *circle of fifths,* the sharp keys occurring clockwise and the flat keys counter-clockwise. The three overlapping keys are said to be *enharmonic,* the choice between one of each pair being a matter of convenience.

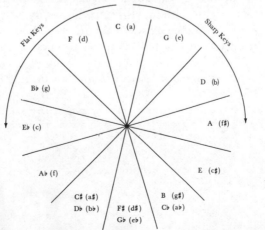

Figure 70

INTERVALS

The *quantitative* name of an interval is determined by counting the number of letter names it contains, including the first and last. This number, which describes the size of an interval in terms of the scale steps it encompasses, is preceded by a *qualitative* term. We found that scales were constructed of *major seconds,* which contain two half steps, or *minor seconds* which contain one half step. While it is possible to define the larger intervals in terms of the number of half steps each contains, it is more convenient to describe them as they relate to the keynote, or *tonic,* of a major scale.

The diatonic intervals as they normally occur up from the tonic of the major scale are called either *major* or *perfect.* Some numerical intervals have *three* possible qualifying descriptive terms, and some have *four.* These must be memorized according to the following chart:

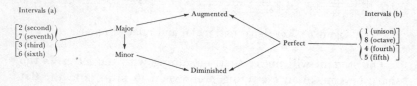

Figure 71

(a) Intervals (left column) that are normally *major* become *augmented* if the distance between the notes is increased one half step; if it is decreased one half step the interval becomes *minor;* if it is further decreased one half step it becomes *diminished.*

(b) Intervals (right column) that are normally *perfect* become *augmented* if the distance between the notes is increased one half step; if it is decreased one half step the interval becomes *diminished.*

Intervals can become *doubly augmented* or *doubly diminished.*

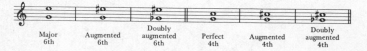

Figure 72

The names of the basic white-key intervals as they occur from the tonic of the C major scale must be memorized.

Practice altering these basic intervals by the addition of accidentals according to the patterns shown in figure 71. For example, name the following intervals:

Figure 74

From this point on the student may use the following abbreviations for the qualifying terms of intervals:

M major
m minor
A augmented
d diminished
P perfect

To correctly name intervals larger than a second, the student first counts the letters to find the quantitative name; the qualitative name is then found according to one of the following methods:

1. Memorize the correct names of the white-key intervals given for the key of C major above; these may then be altered, that is, made larger or smaller by the use of accidentals, according to

figure 71. For example, perfect intervals may be altered as follows:

Figure 75

Imperfect intervals may be altered:

Figure 76

2. When the lower note of an interval is not C, the key signature of the major scale of the lower note must be *imagined*.

Figure 77

If the upper note then occurs as a normal scale degree in the major scale of the lower note, then the interval will be either major or perfect, according to which of the two groups of intervals given in figure 71 it belongs to. If the note is larger or smaller than would normally occur, then the quality of the interval will be determined by the accidental used.

Sometimes it is helpful to check the quality of large intervals by imagining the quality of the complementary small intervals that are more easily seen; for example, the quality of sixths and sevenths will be the opposite of the complementary thirds and seconds.

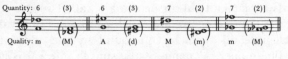

Figure 78

To determine the quality of compound intervals, it is convenient to disregard the octave and to imagine the simple interval.

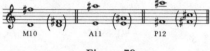

Figure 79

Finally, if the interval utilizes unusual combinations of accidentals, especially double sharps or double flats, it is sometimes convenient to determine the quality of the unaltered notes (letter names) and then make the necessary adjustments.

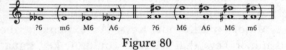

Figure 80

Inversion of Intervals. If the lower tone of an interval is placed an octave higher, or if the upper tone of an interval is placed an octave lower, the interval is said to have been *inverted*. Thus, seconds become sevenths, thirds become sixths and fourths become fifths. (The original interval and its complementary one add up to the number nine.) As for the quality of the interval, perfect remains perfect when inverted, major becomes minor, minor becomes major, augmented becomes diminished, and diminished becomes augmented.

Figure 81

Intervals no larger than an octave are called *simple* intervals, those greater than an octave are called *compound* intervals. Thus any simple interval is made compound by the addition of an octave. (The numerical name of the simple interval is added to the number seven to produce the name of the compound interval.)

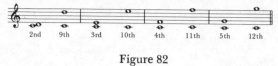

2nd 9th 3rd 10th 4th 11th 5th 12th

Figure 82

RELATIVE, PARALLEL, AND CLOSELY RELATED KEYS

Theorists have given names to certain key relationships that are in common use; these will be defined here, but they will become more important later with the discussion of modulation (the process of changing from one key to another).

Relative Major and Minor Keys. As explained above, the major and minor keys that share a common key signature are termed *relative* (major or minor) keys. For example:

Figure 83

Parallel or Tonic Major (or Minor) Keys. The major and minor keys that share a common keynote or tonic (but not the same key signature) are termed *parallel major* (or *minor*) keys. For example:

Figure 84

Closely Related Keys. The seven-tone major or natural minor scale was expanded (by composers seeking greater tonal variety) by treating each consonant (i.e., major or minor) triad as the keynote of another major or minor key. The diminished triad was eliminated since it could not function as a tonic triad. These six keys were said to be *closely related*.

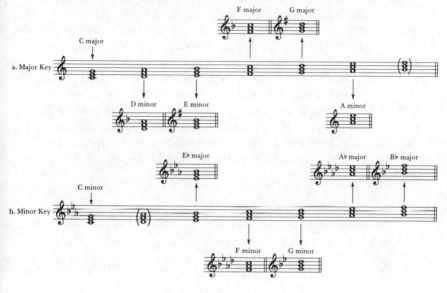

Figure 85

The same set of closely related keys can be defined in two other ways: (1) closely related keys are those which have one more, or one less, accidental in the key signature, and (2) closely related keys are those of the tonic, subdominant, and dominant (the primary scale degrees) and their relatives.

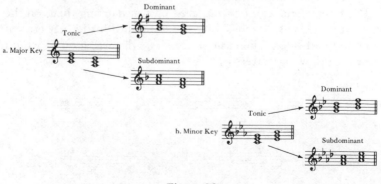

Figure 86

MEDIEVAL CHURCH MODES

In the Middle Ages music was often composed in arrangements of steps and half steps other than those of the major and minor scales; these early scalic patterns were called *modes*. By the sixteenth century this Greater Modal System included seven principal modes (called *authentic*) and seven secondary forms (called *plagal* or *hypo* modes). The plagal forms of the modes, while having the same final, or keynote, as the authentic forms, utilized a different range; since range is no longer a consideration in modern music, we will restrict our discussion to the authentic modes. These have some use in the romantic and contemporary periods, and the following patterns should be noted by the student.

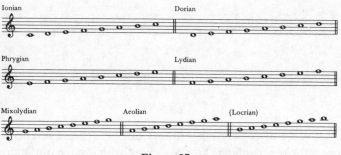

Figure 87

The Ionian and Aeolian modes are like our present major and natural minor scales; the Locrian mode is seldom used because of its diminished tonic chord.

The same modes can be compared by constructing them on the same keynote; this clearly shows the difference in the patterns of steps and half steps. The basic six modes, all starting on C, would show the following patterns:

Figure 88

If the accidentals used in the scales above are assembled into key signatures, the student will see that these differ from those of the conventional major and minor keys. While it would be possible to memorize the step—half step pattern of each of the modes, it is simpler to learn the following design in relation to the C major key signature:

Figure 89

In other words, if one begins upon the second degree of a major scale, this produces the pattern of the Dorian mode, the third degree gives the Phrygian mode, etc. In order to analyze modern modal music (which is frequently transposed), the student must also be able to reverse the process. For example, a composition in two sharps that ends on F sharp is in Phrygian mode; one in three flats that ends on A flat is in Lydian mode, and so on.

WHOLE-TONE SCALES

In romantic and impressionistic music, *whole-tone* scales have some limited use. These are constructed out of six consecutive whole steps. The remaining six tones, of the possible twelve, form a complimentary whole-tone scale. There are only two different whole-tone scales in sound, although these may, of course, be written in several ways.

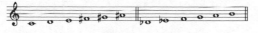

Figure 90

Since the tones are all equidistant, they produce augmented triads and symmetrical four-note chords that are rootless and that quickly induce monotony because of the lack of variety in structure.

Figure 91

PENTATONIC SCALES

The music of Eastern cultures sometimes makes use of *pentatonic,* or *five-tone* scales, which contain no half steps. These scales contain whole steps and minor thirds. They may be constructed in several different ways, but the black keys of the piano show the pattern clearly.

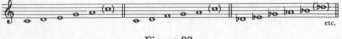

Figure 92

OTHER SCALES

Composers have freely constructed synthetic scales, different from the more usual ones we have reviewed, and folk music sometimes uses peculiar or idiomatic scales. We have discussed the most common scales of five, six, seven, and twelve tones. Synthetic scales may also be constructed to contain eight, nine, and ten tones. Mussorgsky, Debussy, Bartók, and many contemporary composers have consistently made use of unusual scalic combinations. Some possibilities are given below:

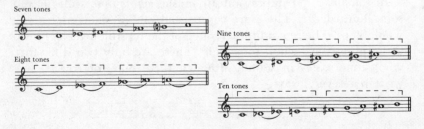

Figure 93

TUNING SYSTEMS AND TEMPERAMENT

At various times in the history of European music different systems have been advanced to calculate intervals and scales. The most important have been:

1. Pythagorean scale
2. Just intonation
3. Mean-tone temperament
4. Equal temperament

Pythagorean Scale. In the sixth century B.C. Pythagoras, a Greek mathematician, is thought to have made certain acoustic experiments with a vibrating string called the *monochord*. By using two monochords, Pythagoras performed an experiment in which the string of one monochord was successively shortened by one half (raising the pitch an octave), and the string of the other was shortened each time by two thirds (raising the pitch a fifth). After seven octaves and twelve fifths, Pythagoras discovered that the B ♯ from the second monochord was not exactly the same as the C produced by the first monochord, but was slightly higher: this small discrepancy is called the *Pythagorean comma*.

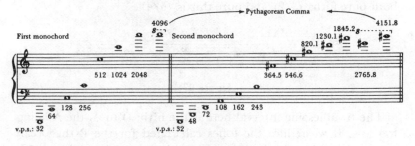

Figure 94

Since all Western European tuning systems are based upon octave equivalence, this small difference, about a ninth of a whole tone, has been a troublesome problem. The tuning systems differ in the manner in which this comma is handled. The so-called Pythagorean scale derives all tones from the interval of the pure fifth (3/2) as it occurs in the overtone series. A diatonic scale can be calculated as a series of five successive upper fifths and one lower fifth, from a given starting point. Using the vibration number 64 to represent C, and calculating by 3/2 (or 2/3), we would have:

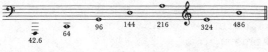

Figure 95

This produces a third, which is considerably higher than the pure third in the overtone series, and makes the system unusable for contrapuntal music.

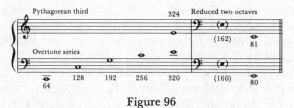

Figure 96

Just Intonation. This system attempts to improve upon the deficiencies of the Pythagorean scale by basing the calculations on both pure fifths (3/2) and pure thirds (5/4).

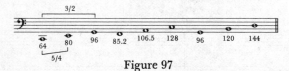

Figure 97

The troublesome interval here is the fifth, D to A, the A being too low. If we reduce the tones calculated for the Pythagorean scale (above) to the lower octave, we can compare these with those from the just intonation scale.

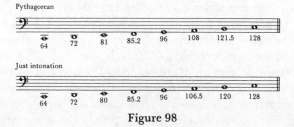

Figure 98

The just intonation scale also multiplies its difficulties as soon as chromatic tones are introduced. String players often are said to be using just intonation when they play sharps higher and flats lower than equal-tempered intervals; however, this is an erroneous conclusion, since, in just intonation, the sharps are actually lower in pitch than the flats.

These and other difficulties caused the pure tuning systems to be abandoned in favor of the tempered systems, whereby the comma could be divided up among several intervals to make it less noticeable.

Mean-Tone Temperament. The mean-tone system of tuning was in use in the sixteenth century especially for keyboard instruments. It is based upon the idea of tempering the third, arrived at by four superimposed fifths, so that it agrees with the pure third from the overtone series. The difference between these two tones—called the *syntonic comma*—is then distributed equally between the four fifths, that is, each fifth is lowered by one quarter of the syntonic comma. The whole tone is thus the mean of the major third.

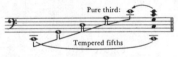

Figure 99

This makes a very usable system of tuning with pure thirds and nearly pure fifths. It worked very well in the renaissance and early baroque periods for keyboard music that did not use key signatures of more than two flats or three sharps; beyond these keys, the introduction of the third flat (A ♭) or the fourth sharp (D ♯), created the problem of an enharmonic tone (A ♭–G ♯, E ♭–D ♯, etc.). Here the system was inadequate, since the enharmonic tones were nearly a quarter of a tone different. The increased use of more distant modulation in baroque music finally led to the abandonment of this system and the introduction of equal temperament.

Equal Temperament. The full development of tonality, from the seven- to the twelve-note scale, forced the choice of a tuning system that could accommodate unlimited modulation and equality of all the twelve pitches. This is made possible by dividing the octave into twelve equal semitones, each of which is slightly tempered. The octave remains the only interval that is pure acoustically, that is, in agreement with the natural overtone series; the fifths are slightly smaller and the thirds somewhat larger than the natural intervals.

A system of measurement has been suggested that assigns 1,200 cents to the octave; each semitone equals 100 cents. For purposes of graphic comparison, it is possible to show the approximate relationships of the diatonic scale in earlier tuning systems in relation to a grid representing the twelve half steps of equal temperament:

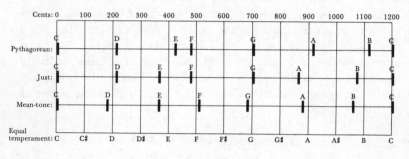

Figure 100

Chapter 4

Chords

Western music uses sonorities of notes sounding together that are called *chords*. Two tones sounding together are usually termed an *interval*, while three or more tones are called a *chord*.

CONSONANCE AND DISSONANCE

In the field of harmony the concepts of *consonance* and *dissonance* usually refer to the stability of the relationships between tones, that is, intervals or chords. This stability is often described as "smooth," "concordant," or "consonant" when the relationship is "pleasant" or "agreeable," or "rough," "discordant," or "dissonant" when the relationship appears to be "unpleasant" or "disagreeable." It is clear that these are subjective judgments and that they vary with individuals and also with cultures and periods.

Western European music, as distinct from that of some Eastern cultures, has generally based the concept of stability upon the norm of the natural harmonic, or overtone, series, which results from a vibrating string or air column. This emphasis upon the harmonic aspect is not found to the same degree in certain Eastern cultures that are melodically oriented. Our sense of consonance, concordance, or agreement comes from the lowest six tones of the overtone series that produce a major triad.

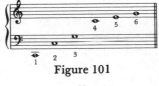

Figure 101

49

These tones give us the intervals of the octave, perfect fifth, perfect fourth, and the major and minor thirds. Of course, if one continues with the overtone series, all tones and intervals would eventually appear (as well as some that are not in our tempered system), and this suggests that consonance and dissonance are simply relative terms, rather than absolutes.

This view is also borne out by history, since in the Middle Ages, when octaves, fourths, and fifths were "consonant," the third was considered "dissonant." Later, after 1450, we developed a norm of tertian harmony based upon the triad.

The usual characterization of consonant and dissonant intervals in the "common-practice period" (1700–1900) is shown by this chart:

Perfect consonance   Imperfect consonance   Dissonance

P1 P8 P5 P4   M3 m6 m3 M6   M2 m7 m2 M7 d5 A4

Figure 102

However, it is more realistic today to say that consonance and dissonance are relative, rather than absolute, terms; they are different degrees of the same thing.

Intervals are also said to have *roots;* the mind seeks a focal point for an interval or a complex chord. We seek the strongest, most important tone as the root of the interval or chord. While there are complex acoustic and stylistic reasons for choosing roots, the following chart shows the gradation of stability in two-part intervals and the generally accepted roots (→) .

Stable   Unstable

Consonant   Dissonant

Figure 103

The octave represents complete agreement, while the *tritone,* or augmented fourth, sets up two different overtone series that conflict with each other and therefore make the interval seem rootless.

Three intervals require special mention. During the period of triadic harmony, the interval of the perfect fourth *with the bass note,* or the lowest sounding note in a chord, was considered a dissonance. This "conceptual dissonance" was based upon the disagreement that the fourth makes with the strong overtone of the major third from the lowest tone.

Figure 104

This is the basis for treating the six-four ($^6_4$) chord as a dissonant combination, requiring resolution to a five-three ($^5_3$) chord during this period.

Figure 105

Fourths between *upper parts* were not considered dissonant and so required no resolution.

Augmented fifths were also considered to be dissonant. While this interval is acoustically the same as the minor sixth, when it is part of an augmented triad it is perceived as an altered tone. Early nineteenth-century theorists considered this to be a "frozen" passing tone that ultimately required resolution.

Figure 106

During this period all *augmented* and *diminished* intervals were considered dissonant (A4, d5, A5, d8, A2, d7, and so on) .

Finally there is the enigma of the minor third, which is treated as a "consonance." The minor third above a bass tone "disagrees" with the overtone series of the lower tone in the same way as that described above for the perfect fourth; however, the minor third became an acceptable consonance which required no resolution.

Figure 107

During the sixteenth century conservative composers like Palestrina were reluctant to end a composition on this "dissonance." This probably accounts for the *tierce de Picardie* (Picardy third), the practice of ending a composition in a minor mode upon a major triad. Hindemith, among others, believes that we accept the minor third as consonance because we perceive it as a "darker" version of the natural overtone.

Triads: root position and inversions

The first six notes of the natural overtone series produce a composite sound that we call the *major triad*. This basic sonority became the pattern for the system of triadic harmony, that is, the construction of chords out of superimposed thirds. Sonorities that contain three different tones in superimposed thirds are called *triads;* those chords of four or more tones are named for the largest interval they contain.

Figure 108

Since the spaces between tones vary, constructing triads on different tones of the scale will produce triads of different types.

Four basic triad types are generally recognized and have been given convenient labels: major, minor, diminished, and augmented.

Figure 109

The *major* and *minor* triads are consonant; they contain major and minor thirds and a perfect fifth. The *diminished* and *augmented* triads are dissonant, since they contain the intervals of diminished and augmented fifths, as well as thirds.

The members of triads are named as follows:

Figure 110

The student should practice constructing all of the triad types on different pitches.

The triad is in *root position* when the root of the triad is the bass, or lowest-sounding tone. Triads may be *inverted* by placing the lowest-sounding tone an octave higher. The *first inversion* has the third of the chord as the bass, or lowest tone; the *second inversion* has the fifth as the bass.

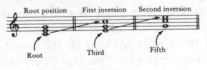

Figure 111

SEVENTH CHORDS AND LARGER STRUCTURES IN SUPERIMPOSED THIRDS

Early contrapuntal music used consonant triads as the basis for its harmonic material; these sonorities were elaborated by certain dissonant nonharmonic tones (see Chapter 13). After 1600 some nonharmonic devices, such as passing tones and suspensions, began to be incorporated into the basic sonorities as chord members.

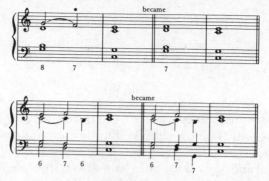

Figure 112

This resulted in the recognition of dissonant *seventh* chords as independent harmonies, though still requiring resolution of the dissonant member. There are several different types of seventh chords, depending upon which scale degree is the root of the chord. These may be labeled or symbolized with two letters, the first indicating the type of triad, the second the type of seventh (see Chapter 5); if the two letters are the same, only one is used.

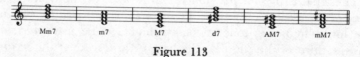

Figure 113

The nineteenth-century composers continued the process of superimposing thirds; this resulted in *ninth* chords and, late in the romantic period, *eleventh* and *thirteenth* chords. The names are derived from the largest interval in the chord and, like the seventh chords, several types are possible. There is no universally accepted system for symbolizing all of the possible types, but those constructed on V, II, and I are the most used. It is, of course, possible to chromatically alter members of these chords.

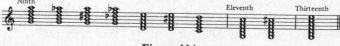

Figure 114

When these larger chords are used in piano or orchestral music it is possible to have them complete, but when they are used in a four-part vocal texture certain less important tones have to be omitted. These larger chords are most common in root position; inversions occur less frequently. In four-voice texture the following are common distributions:

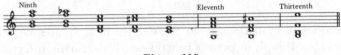

Ninth   Eleventh   Thirteenth

Figure 115

OTHER CHORD STRUCTURES (FOURTHS, FIFTHS, SECONDS, AND SO ON)

Late romantic and contemporary composers experimented with other kinds of chord structures, that is, harmonies were constructed by superimposing other intervals than thirds. At the beginning of this century Scriabin used a *mystic chord* constructed from various kinds of fourths as the basis for his symphonic poem *Prometheus* and for other compositions.

Figure 116

It is clear from the sound that the notation in fourths (both augmented and diminished) is misleading; this chord sounds like one of the larger dominant chords with lowered fifth.

When the chord is constructed all of perfect fourths, the effect is quite different; fourth chords may contain from three to six or more tones.

Figure 117

Somewhat similar in sound are chords built in perfect fifths (the inversion of fourths) .

Figure 118

Composers from Debussy to Hindemith have frequently made use of chords built of perfect fourths or fifths, usually integrating them into a style that is still fundamentally triadic and tonal. These chords, like all other chords that are built of equal intervals (for example, augmented triads and diminished seventh chords) have a certain sameness of sonority that quickly leads to monotony unless they are used along with other, less symmetrical chord types. Since they are all built of equal intervals, they sound rootless; or to be more accurate, when the isolated chord does not have a strong acoustical root, the apparent root must be determined by the use in the musical context.

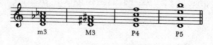

Figure 119

The only interval left from which symmetrical chord structures might be built is the second. This produces what are generally called *tone clusters*. Henry Cowell, among others, has made tone clusters of different sizes a feature of his piano music. These are frequently notated with a bar connecting the extremes of the intended chord and are played with the fingers, hand, or arm.

Figure 120

On the piano, because of the construction of the keyboard, some seconds will be major and some minor, if just the white keys are used; in the orchestra, tone clusters can be written using all major or all minor seconds.

In the history of music, far more often than the symmetrical chord types just discussed, composers have used sonorities built of a combination of different intervals. While any conceivable combination might occur, for purposes of catagorization, it is convenient to relate sonorities to some already designated type. This has led to a concept of *added tones,* that is, notes added to a conventional triad, seventh, or fourth chord. Popular music and jazz use the added sixth to both the major and minor triads without changing the basic chord function, and Debussy was fond of the added sixth and ninth.

Figure 121

The practice of adding tones has finally led to the superimposing of one chord upon another. Stravinsky and others have frequently opposed tonic and dominant formations.

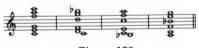

Figure 122

These bichordal combinations have frequently led to what is called *bitonality,* that is, the suggestion of two keys. This term must be interpreted loosely to cover not only two "keys" but also the superimposing of various chord types.

Figure 123

One must study examples from music literature to see how composers have used the various sonority types that have been enumerated here. To see how composers in different periods used these chords is to undertake a detailed study of musical style. However, as a very general principle, one can say that the more complex, colorful, and disssonant chords—seventh, ninth, fourth chords, added tones, etc.—have, throughout the tonal period, often been used as more intense substitutes for the simple, functional triads.

Chapter 5

Symbolization

Music theory has developed a symbolization that is particularly useful in discussing, or analyzing, music in the absence of staff notation. While the details of this vary from one theory book to another, the following seem to be the most useful concepts that have the greatest agreement.

BASIC SYMBOLS AND DEFINITIONS

Letters are often used to symbolize the quality of intervals and chords.

> M major
> m minor
> A augmented
> d diminished
> P perfect

These qualitative symbols may be combined with the quantitative numbers to indicate intervals: P5, A4, m6, M3, d5, and so on.

The first four letters (M, m, A, d) may also be used to abbreviate triad types.

To describe the sonority of seventh chords two terms are used; the first refers to the type of triad, the second to the kind of seventh. When two like letters occur they are combined.

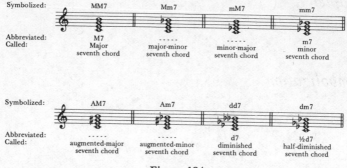

Figure 124

NAMES OF SCALE DEGREES AND CHORDS

Scale degrees, and the chords constructed upon them, are frequently identified by names and numbers. Arabic numbers are used to identify scale degrees, which are the same in both major and minor keys. The names are the same in both major and minor, with the exception of those for the seventh degree; the unaltered seventh degree of the natural minor scale is sometimes called the *subtonic,* while the raised seventh degree is called the *leading tone,* as in the major scale.

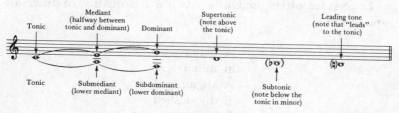

Figure 125

Scale Degree	Name
1.	Tonic
2.	Supertonic
3.	Mediant
4.	Subdominant
5.	Dominant
6.	Submediant
7.	Leading tone (or subtonic)

These names also apply to the chords constructed upon these scale degrees. Roman numerals are used to symbolize these chords (See Roman Numeral Chord Symbol—Functional Harmony, p. 63).

FIGURED BASS

In the early baroque period a system of musical shorthand was developed to make the writing of keyboard parts easier. The usual practice was to write out the bass line and to place, above or below it, arabic numerals indicating the harmonies. The actual keyboard part, or *continuo* as it was called, was then improvised by the player from this guide. While practices have differed slightly in different periods, the general principles are clear and have become fairly well standardized. The student should keep in mind that this type of symbolization is usually predicated upon the performer's seeing the bass note; the exception to this, where figured bass numerals are combined with the roman-numeral chord symbol for the purpose of analysis, is discussed below.

In the practice of figured bass, arabic numerals show the intervals sounding above a given bass part. Simple, rather than compound, intervals are used, since there is no attempt to show in which voice a particular interval occurs nor the precise octave in which it sounds. Exceptions: 9 8 may be used instead of 2 1, and 7 8 9 rather than 7 1 2. For simultaneous sounding tones the figures are arranged vertically, with the largest figure at the top. Certain abbreviations have become well established; the student should use these rather than the complete figuration, unless some ambiguity would result.

The customary abbreviations are these:

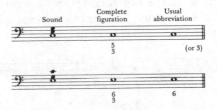

Figure 126

Alterations from the printed key signature are indicated by placing the appropriate accidental before the arabic numeral.

Figure 127

Two abbreviations of this principle have been sanctioned by long usage. They are:

1. An accidental that is not followed by a figure refers to the third above the bass note. The previous example might also have been written:

Figure 128

2. A diagonal stroke placed through a figure, from upper right to lower left, may be used to indicate an interval that is raised a chromatic half step. The previous example could also be written:

Figure 129

Melodic motion in upper parts should be shown by the figures. While no attempt is made to show exact rhythmic values, the figures should show the relative position of the upper parts by spacing and vertical alignment.

A dash is used to show that a tone is held or repeated. For example:

Figure 130

To avoid confusion with a root-position chord, a nonharmonic tone that occurs in the bass voice should be figured, or the continuation of the previous chord indicated by dashes.

Figure 131

ROMAN NUMERAL CHORD SYMBOLS: FUNCTIONAL HARMONY

In the early nineteenth century, German theorists began to use roman numerals to symbolize functional harmony; that is, in conventional tonality, the function of a tonic or a dominant chord was symbolized by I or V. Two kinds of systems developed. One utilized large roman numerals, representing the scale degree upon which the chord was built, for all triad types in both major and minor keys.

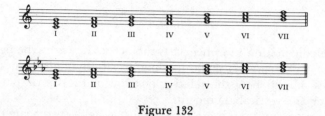

Figure 132

The other system utilized separate symbols for each triad type. For example, the major, minor, diminished, and augmented triads were symbolized by large numerals, small numerals, small numerals with a circle, and large numerals with a cross, respectively.

Figure 133

While some theory books still use this latter system, it is not recommended, since no real advantage is afforded by using different symbols for the four triad types, and this system becomes unwieldy when it is extended to chromatically altered seventh and ninth chords.

Since scale degrees are numbered in relation to a tonic, this point of reference must first be established. Some theorists write out the name of the major or minor key, but we will use the following symbols: capital letters will represent major keys; lower-case letters will indicate minor keys. If the keynote is an altered tone, the accidental will follow the letter. A colon is placed after the key indication.

$$
\begin{array}{rl}
\text{C:} & \text{Key of C major} \\
\text{c:} & \text{Key of C minor} \\
\text{B}\flat: & \text{Key of B flat major} \\
\text{f}\sharp: & \text{Key of F sharp minor}
\end{array}
$$

The addition of a 7 to the upper right of the roman numeral adds that diatonic interval to the diatonic triad. A similar symbolization may be used for ninth, eleventh, and thirteenth chords.

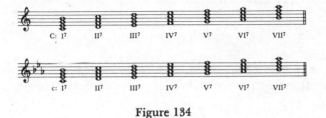

Figure 134

Some theory books advocate calling VII and VII⁷ "incomplete dominant seventh and ninth cords" (V°_{7} and V°_{9}), because these chords on the leading tone frequently resolve to the tonic, as the dominant chords do. Since this leads to unnecessary speculation about "missing" chord members, we will symbolize these with VII and VII⁷, in the same manner as all other chords.

The exact inversion of a triad or seventh chord may be shown by combining the correct figures from figured bass with the roman numeral. These are placed to the right of the roman numeral, beginning with the largest figure at the upper right corner and continuing downward.

$$
\text{I}^{6} \qquad \text{II}^{6}_{4} \qquad \text{V}^{4}_{3} \qquad \text{V}^{6}_{4\ 2}
$$

Any alteration, different from the diatonic version of the chord, also can be shown by the chord symbol. While many special systems have been devised to show alterations, these systems are superfluous, since we already have the well-established system of figured bass (see p. 61). Exactly the same accidentals and figures used in figured bass are combined with the roman numeral. However, to avoid any confusion, it is recommended that an accidental not be used alone, but should always be followed by the figure 3; the use of the diagonal stroke (/) is *not* recommended here. Alterations to the third, fifth, or seventh of a *root position* chord would be indicated:

Figure 135

If the root of a root position chord is altered, this is shown by placing the proper accidental *before* the roman numeral.

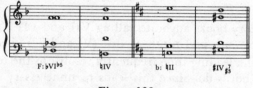

Figure 136

If a chord occurs in an inversion, the same arabic figuration used for figured bass will be added to the roman numeral. Note the fourth chord below; if the root is altered but the chord is inverted, the accidental will not precede the roman numeral as in root position, but will precede the proper figure.

Figure 137

When the bass note of an *inverted* chord is altered with an accidental this may be shown with the figure 1.

Figure 138

This takes care of all of the usual alterations within a key; however, certain additional problems in harmonic symbolization occur when a "new key" is established—that is, when a *modulation* takes place. The concept of modulation, as the process of changing key, is discussed in Chapter 7. The student is referred to that chapter if the concept requires clarification; however, the *symbolization* of the process of modulation will be discussed here.

When a common-chord modulation takes place, the chord (or, sometimes, chords) that is common to both keys, called the *pivot* chord, is given a dual analysis; one shows how the chord is approached in the old key and the other how it is left in the new key. The roman numeral symbols for the new key should be placed on a different level. A difficulty arises in symbolizing those tones in the new key which are "diatonic," or unaltered, in that key, but which require accidentals because the old key signature is still in effect. For example:

Figure 139. J. S. Bach, Chorale no. 298, "Weg, mein Herz, mit den Gedanken"

Most theory books would analyze the above phrase as beginning in the key of C major, and modulating to the key of G major (the dominant). The roman numerals would be:

Figure 140

In terms of these symbols the entire process looks "diatonic," that is, the symbols show no alterations. The figured bass symbols are more realistic; they show that, in relation to the basic key, some alteration has taken place. Therefore, in keeping with our basic premise that the figures and accidentals from figured bass be combined with the roman numeral symbol in order to show the inversions and alterations, we recommend the following: when a modulation takes place, the roman numeral symbol will show all alterations that occur in relation to the printed key signature. The phrase would then be analyzed as follows:

Figure 141

For additional clarity, the chromatically altered tones that would be "diatonic" in the new key are placed in parentheses. This analysis keeps the focus upon the original key by enumerating those alterations which are necessary to emphasize the new, temporary tonal center.

In a chromatic or direct modulation, the symbolization of a pivot chord is often dispensed with in favor of going directly to the new key. While it is always possible to show a pivot-chord analysis in both keys, sometimes the connection is not strongly functional, or is obscure, and it is better to omit it. For example:

Figure 142. J. S. Bach, Chorale no. 139, "Warum sollt' ich mich denn grämen"

At (*A*) the pivot chord is given a dual analysis, since **II** and **VI** are both functional, and the chromatic motion produces an altered chord (minor subdominant chord) in the new key of C major. For the chromatic modulation at (*B*) no common chord is shown, since the first chord still functions as V of C, while the second chord is the V with raised leading tone in A minor. The first chord could be called a natural VII in A minor, but this is not especially meaningful in the minor key. Also, in the direct modulation at (*C*) the dual symbolization of the first chord is dropped in favor of beginning the phrase directly in the new key of G major. The first chord at (*C*) could be called a natural V in A minor, but again, this is more theoretical than strongly functional.

The symbols derived from figured bass and the roman numerals are especially useful when, in the absence of staff notation, one must analyze music or discuss musical concepts.

CHORD SYMBOLS IN POPULAR MUSIC AND JAZZ

Popular songs and jazz arrangements frequently supplement the staff notation by the addition of chord symbols placed over the melody; these are usually associated with the guitar or piano parts, or the sheet-music editions for voice and piano.

While there are small differences between particular publishers, the general principles of the symbolization are clear.

Letter names (followed by an accidental, where appropriate) signify a major triad built upon that root, regardless of any printed key signature. The notation is completely enharmonic, but for major triads flats are more common than sharps.

Figure 143

Minor, augmented, and diminished chords are shown by the letter name of the chord root plus one of the following abbreviations:

m, mi, or min   minor triad
+ or aug   augmented triad
dim   diminished seventh chord (the diminished triad
                is not used)

Figure 144

Jazz harmony often is consistently four part, that is, in place of a triad the chord of the *added sixth* will be used. The major sixth is added to either the major or minor triad and symbolized by the addition of the figure 6.

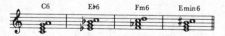

Figure 145

The addition of the figure 7 adds a *minor seventh* to any of the symbols for triads.

Figure 146

The addition of the *major seventh* occurs only with the major triad and is symbolized:

Figure 147

The alteration of the fifth in the seventh chord is shown by a plus sign (+) for raised and a minus sign (−), or a flat (♭) for lowered.

Figure 148

Ninth chords are either of the dominant or tonic types, with the necessary alterations shown.

Figure 149

Occasionally the eleventh or thirteenth is added to the dominant seventh chord, and this is shown by the appropriate figures. Other sonorities, which are not made from superimposed thirds, are shown as *added tones*. For example:

Figure 150

Usually the bass note for any jazz chord is the root of the chord indicated; when this is not the case, that is, when an inversion is intended, that indication is added to the chord symbol.

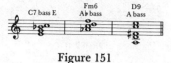

Figure 151

In some school classes an instrument called the autoharp is used to provide a chordal accompaniment for folk songs. Above the melody line for such printed songs, it is usual to indicate the chord for the autoharp; exactly the same chord symbols are used as those just described for jazz, but only simple triads and the dominant seventh chord are possible.

Chapter 6

Expression Marks and Foreign-Language Terms

During the baroque period, Italian composers began the practice of using words to supplement staff notation. These words were like rubrics, which gave additional clarification to the composer's intent. Since that time these Italian terms have been used in the printed music of many countries and have generally been adopted as a kind of international vocabulary concerning music.

In more recent times, romantic and contemporary composers in many countries have chosen to make their explanatory remarks in their own language. One finds Wagner's comments in German, Debussy's in French, Ives's in English, and Prokofiev's in Russian. This has led to the necessity of musicians having a working vocabulary in Italian, French, German, and English, and to some confusion about terms in such lesser-known languages as Russian and Hungarian.

We will give a basic vocabulary of the most useful terms in Italian; the student may consult dictionaries or other standard reference works for the meaning of terms in other languages.

TEMPO

The most accurate way to show the *tempo*, or actual rate of speed, of the basic pulsation is to use the metronomic indications that were given in Chapter 2. These show the number of beats per minute for some basic note value; ($\quad = 60$) means that the quarter note represents the beat and that there are 60 beats per minute (or 1 beat per second).

In addition, there is usually a term to indicate the approximate speed. The following are the most common, arranged from slow to fast:

Largo	Very slow
Larghetto	Not as slow as *largo*
Adagio	Slow
Lento	Slow
Moderato	Moderate
Andante	"Going"—with moderate motion
Andantino	Faster than *andante*
Allegretto	Less fast than *allegro*
Allegro	Moderately fast
Vivace	Vivacious, fast
Presto	Fast
Prestissimo	Very fast

The following terms, arranged alphabetically, represent *changes* in the basic tempo:

Accelerando	(*accel.*)	Accelerating
Allargando	(*allarg.*)	Broadening, slowing down
Fermata	(⌢)	To hold (literally, "stopped")
Rallentando	(*rall.*)	Slowing down
Ritardando	(*ritard.*)	Slowing, or holding back
	(*rit.*)	
Ritenuto	(*rit.*)	Held back
Rubato		Freely (literally, "robbed")
Stringendo	(*string.*)	Speeding up

DYNAMICS

These terms refer to the dynamic level at which the music is to be played, and are arranged from soft to loud:

Pianissimo	(*pp*)	Very soft
Piano	(*p*)	Soft
Mezzo piano	(*mp*)	Moderately soft
Mezzo forte	(*mf*)	Moderately loud
Forte	(*f*)	Loud
Fortissimo	(*ff*)	Very loud

This scale will occasionally be extended from *ppp* to *fff*. *Changes* in the dynamic level are indicated by:

Crescendo	(*cresc.*)	Increasing in volume	
Decrescendo	(*decresc.*)	Decreasing in volume	
Diminuendo	(*dim.*)	Diminishing	
Rinforzando	(*rfz*)	Reinforcing	
Sforzando	(*sfz*)	Forcing	

STYLE

The general manner or style in which the music is to be played is indicated by such terms as the following:

Animato	Animated
Cantabile	In a singing style
Dolce	Sweetly
Espressivo	Expressive
Grazioso	Graceful
Legato	Smoothly, connected
Maestoso	Majestic
Marcato	Marked
Semplice	Simply
Solo	One, alone
Sostenuto	Sustained
Staccato	Short, detached
Tenuto	Long, held for full value
Tutti	All, together

The following terms may be used to modify, or further clarify, the basic terms (for example, *Allegro assai* = very fast), or give additional directions for performance:

Ad libitum (*ad lib*.)	At will
Assai	Very
Con brio	With brilliance
L'istesso tempo	Same tempo
Meno mosso	Slower (literally, "less moved")
Molto	Very or much
Non tanto	Not so much
Non troppo	Not too much
Più mosso	Faster (literally "more moved")
Poco	Little
Poco a poco	Little by little
Quasi	Almost or as if
Segue	Follows
Sempre	Always
Simile	Similarly
Sotto voce	Subdued voice
Subito	Suddenly
Volta subito	Turn over quickly

PHRASING AND ARTICULATION

Melodies may be performed in different ways, that is, they may be played *legato* (smoothly), *marcato* (marked), *staccato* (detached), and so on. In addition to general terms, there are specific signs used in conjunction with notation to indicate phrasing and articulation. Unfortunately, there is no universal agreement among instrumentalists as to the exact meaning of these signs; a sign may mean something slightly different when used for different instruments (that is, piano, string instruments, or wind instruments). More particular treatment concerned with bowing, tonguing, and so on, must be left to the study of orchestration.

Slurs. Different from a tie, which connects notes of the same pitch, the *slur* is a curved line, placed above or below notes, to indicate they are to be played in a smooth, connected way.

Figure 152

While such a slur frequently is intended to show a musical phrase, slurs may also be used to show more detailed articulation.

Figure 153

Dots. A *dot* placed above or below the note head means that the note is to be played short.

Figure 154

Dashes. *Dashes* (tenuto marks) indicate that notes are to be played long, that is, they are to be articulated but held for their full value.

Figure 155

Accents. Dynamic *accents* are usually indicated by placing the following signs over or under the notes:

Figure 156

Wedges. The *wedge* that points up (also printed as ▼) usually indicates a note that is both accented and short. This is customarily not used with a note of long value.

Figure 157

Combinations. When slurs are found under a slur, the longer slur indicates a musical phrase, while the smaller slurs show the articulation.

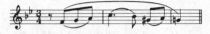

Figure 158

When dots and dashes are placed under a slur there is less general agreement as to what this means, but usually it indicates a detached or semi-legato style.

Figure 159

ABBREVIATIONS

D.C., an abbreviation for *da capo* (from the beginning), and D.S., an abbreviation for *dal segno* (from the sign), mean to repeat the music from the beginning or from this sign: 𝄋 . When the sign 𝄌 is found, it usually means to go to the *coda*, or the closing section of music.

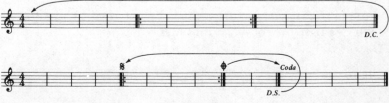

Figure 160

In making D.C. and D.S. returns, repeat marks within the section are ignored the second time.

A repeated measure is shown by this sign:

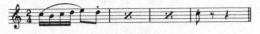

Figure 161

The repetition of two measures may be indicated:

Figure 162

Repeated figures within the bar may be shown by diagonal slashes, the number of strokes equaling the number of note beams.

Figure 163

A long note value may be broken up into eighth, sixteenth or thirty-second notes by the proper number of slashes above the note or through the stem; the value of the longer note is played in eighths or sixteenths, and so on.

Figure 164

If an unmeasured tremolo is desired, four slashes should be used:

Figure 165

An unmeasured legato tremolo or trill between two pitches may be indicated similarly, but notice that each pitch is written with the whole value of its group.

Figure 166

FOREIGN NAMES FOR SCALE DEGREES AND KEYS

In foreign publications of music, scale degrees and keys often appear, particularly in titles of compositions, in the language of the country.

NAMES OF NOTES OR SCALE DEGREES

English		*Italian*	*French*	*German*
C	(C)	do	ut	C
C sharp	(C♯)	do diesis	ut dièse	Cis
D flat	(D♭)	re bemolle	ré bémol	Des
D	(D)	re	ré	D
D sharp	(D♯)	re diesis	ré dièse	Dis
E flat	(E♭)	mi bemolle	mi bémol	Es
E	(E)	mi	mi	E
E sharp	(E♯)	mi diesis	mi dièse	Eis
F flat	(F♭)	fa bemolle	fa bémol	Fes
F	(F)	fa	fa	F
F sharp	(F♯)	fa diesis	fa dièse	Fis
G flat	(G♭)	sol bemolle	sol bémol	Ges
G	(G)	sol	sol	G
G sharp	(G♯)	sol diesis	sol dièse	Gis

A flat	(A ♭)	la bemolle	la bémol	As
A	(A)	la	la	A
A sharp	(A ♯)	la diesis	la dièse	Ais
B flat	(B ♭)	si bemolle	si bémol	B
B	(B)	si	si	H
B sharp	(B ♯)	si diesis	si dièse	His
C flat	(C ♭)	do bemolle	ut bémol	Ces

NAMES OF KEYS

| major | *maggiore* | *majeur* | *dur* |
| minor | *minore* | *mineur* | *moll* |

Part II
Tonal Harmony

Chapter 7

Tonality and Key Feeling

The term *tonality* has two generally accepted definitions: (1) in its most general use it simply means music which has a tonic, that is, music which exhibits an organizational affinity for an all-important center, or *keynote*; (2) in its more specific and narrow sense it means a tonal organization synonymous with the major-minor key system of the eighteenth and nineteenth centuries.

We will discuss the more general use of the term first, since all music, whatever its period or style, has a tonic, with the possible exception of some recent atonal music, which purposely attempts to avoid this.

TONALITY

In order to abstract meaning out of complexity, the human mind seeks some form of simplification. The history of Western music shows several instances in which the mind chooses a single tone to represent a *klang*, or collection, of many different sounds. The *root* of an interval, or complex chord, the *finalis* of a mode, the *tonic* of a key, or the *fundamental* of the natural overtone series, these all exhibit the same hierarchical principle in which we seek to single out one all-important element to represent several others.

Figure 167

In all of these cases, where two or more different tones occur, we tend to focus our attention upon the most important tone. In the case of an interval or chord, we say the important tone is the *root;* where more tones are associated, as in a scale or key, we say that the center is the *tonic.*

The basic question then becomes: what prompts us to choose one tone, rather than another, as the root, tonic, or tonal center? Hindemith[1] assigns roots to intervals or chords largely on the basis of an acoustical phenomenon, that is, by deciding which tone is best supported by the overtone structure. However, in the case of a key or tonal area, other factors must be considered, particularly the one of *emphasis.* The tonal organization must emphasize, or focus our attention upon, the tonic of the composition.

This emphasis is accomplished by different means in different periods. In monophonic music the tonal center is established by melodic means. This is done largely by circling around a particular tone *(neighbor-note motion)*, that is, the tonic or finalis is reached by a stepwise motion. These formulas of conclusion are called *cadences.*

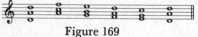

Figure 168

In early contrapuntal music, each voice reached its goal by melodic means, while the vertical combinations laid the foundation for harmony.

Figure 169

In the thirteenth and fourteenth centuries this cadential action was intensified by the use of accidentals *(musica ficta)*, which made the *leading tone* closer to the note it resolved to. Sometimes the inner part also used an *auxiliary leading tone.*

Figure 170

[1] Paul Hindemith, *The Craft of Musical Composition* (New York: Associated Music Publishers, 1945) .

In a typical fifteenth-century cadence, the crossing of the inner part produces a sonority like the later "dominant" function, while still allowing the two more important outer parts to approach the final by step.

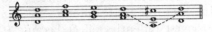

Figure 171

The reaching of the final note by stepwise motion in both parts is still called *clausula vera* (true cadence) in the sixteenth century.

Figure 172

In certain scalic patterns (the Phrygian mode, for example) the leading tone principle is inverted, that is, one part moves by the interval of a half step down, instead of up.

Figure 173

With the increase in the number of parts, from two or three to four or more, the individuality of the many separate lines had to be subordinated to the overall harmonic progression. When the chord progression contains sonorities of three or four different tones, we seek the roots of those chords as a guide to the overall organization. In the eighteenth century, Rameau advocated writing out, on a separate staff below the music, the roots of the chords, which he called the *fundamental bass*.

In examining this root movement, we may disregard interval inversion and reduce the harmonic progression of roots to those a fifth, third, or second apart, or to repeated chords.

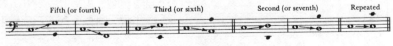

Figure 174

Roots a fifth apart produce the strongest sense of harmonic progression. Contrary to melodic cadential patterns, which emphasize the strong melodic interval of a second, the strongest harmonic cadences, the *authentic* or *full,* and the *plagal* cadence, use root movements of the fifth, or its inversion, the fourth.

If we examine the authentic cadence, we can see that this produces the strongest cadential effect because it combines the strong melodic movement of the *clausula vera* with the strong root movement of a fifth.

V   I

Figure 175

The plagal cadence is a less dynamic final cadence. It combines stepwise motion with the root movement of the fourth, but the common tone softens the cadential effect.

IV   I

Figure 176

Here is a Bach chorale with the abstracted roots of the vertical harmonies. This fundamental bass will tell us something about the tonality, or how the music is organized.

G

Figure 177. J. S. Bach, Chorale no. 168, "Heut'ist, o Mensch, ein grosser"

The roots of the chords for this chorale tell us that G is the tonic; the chorale begins on G, it modulates (see Modulation, p. 94) to the relative major, B flat—Heinrich Schenker (see p. 99) would say that the third of the tonic chord is emphasized—and it returns to G. We understand this tonal organization from the root movement, not from the key signature nor the content of the scale. To be more precise about stylistic details, we could say that this is an ancient modal melody (transposed Dorian mode, if one believes the key signature, or transposed Aeolian, if one counts the E flat) harmonized by Bach in the eighteenth-century style of a minor key, and ending with a Picardy third. The tabulation of the root movement would be:

Chords a fifth apart:	18
Chords a second apart:	8
Chords a third apart:	2
Repeated chords:	2

In addition to the strong harmonic focus upon G at the beginning and end of the chorale, we can also see that the melody itself is an elaboration of the notes in the tonic chord.

Figure 178

Emphasis produced by cadential patterns, whether melodic or harmonic, is possibly the strongest factor in establishing a tonic. Less important is scalic content, as was shown by the choral phrase above. While there is a strong tendency, in analyzing harmonic music from the last two hundred years, to assume that the key signature tells us the tonic, we know from past experience with modal scales that this may not be so. In other words, with any given key signature or collection of pitches, the composer can choose any one of several pitches and, by emphasis, make it the tonal center. The four authentic medieval church modes used the same pitches, but, by melodic emphasis, were able to achieve different finals.

Figure 179

Root movements of seconds and thirds produce less emphatic progressions, and these are normally used for interior progressions and cadences rather than final ones.

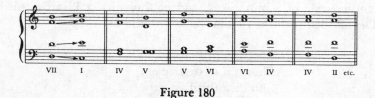

Figure 180

For a fuller discussion of the different types of cadences, the student may refer to Chapter 11.

In addition to the strength of the root movement and the emphasis of cadential formulas, the following factors may also affect the determination of a tonic: stress or accent, duration, the tone most frequently repeated or returned to, and the resolution of dissonance to consonance. Tension followed by relaxation is a characteristic of many types of cadence. We say that the concept of tonic represents a point of rest or repose, therefore the consonant triad, or the less dissonant chord, assumes the role of a tonic when it is preceded by a greater dissonance.

Figure 181

Of the several factors mentioned above that aid in establishing a tonic, in a given situation one may conflict with another. Which of these factors takes precedence over the others can be decided only by the individual context, and this must be left to the analysis of a particular piece of music.

KEY FEELING

To many musicians, the key feeling of a major or minor scale is synonymous with the idea of tonality. While this is too narrow a concept of tonality, it is, nevertheless, a view that is valid for much music of the eighteenth and nineteenth centuries.

By the middle of the baroque period most of the vestiges of modality had disappeared in favor of a more standardized major or minor key. It would be more accurate to say that *musica ficta,* especially the raised leading tone in the cadence, had reduced the various modal scales to one of two patterns, depending upon the type of third in the final chord. The second tetrachord in all of the church modes became identical, except for the Phrygian mode.

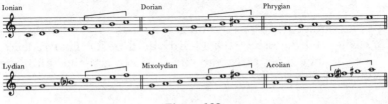

Figure 182

The Phrygian mode did not conform to the pattern because of the interval of the half step between the first and second scale degrees. The seventh degree in this mode could not be raised in the traditional cadence without producing an augmented sixth, a dissonant interval.

Figure 183

This peculiarity made possible the so-called *Phrygian cadence,* popular in the eighteenth century, in which the bass voice progressed down a half step.

Figure 184

The distinction between all of the other modes disappeared, and one spoke only of a major mode, or a minor mode, depending upon the type of tonic chord.

Figure 185

The various forms of the minor scale—natural, harmonic, and melodic—and the use of the Picardy third in the final cadence, gave the minor key three variable scale degrees; the third, the sixth, and seventh degrees were frequently raised.

Figure 186

By the beginning of the nineteenth century, this amalgamation had produced a composite that might be called the *major–minor scale*. This ten-tone scale was organized by a system of functional harmony in which the quality or color of the primary functions could be varied without disturbing the feeling for tonic.

Figure 187

The seven-tone modal scales, which since the medieval period had used seven letter-names or syllables for purposes of notation, now were expanded into a ten-tone major–minor key. This was only an intermediate step toward the twelve-tone scale, which was reached by the middle of the nineteenth century, and for which the seven-letter notation began to be clearly inadequate.

Tonality, or key-feeling, in this common-practice period comes from the root movement, which sets up a tonic, rather than from the color of the chords used. The seven-tone scale key signature was still used, but it was practically meaningless, since any number of tones from seven to twelve could be used without disturbing the basic key-feeling, so long as the root movement focused upon the tonic.

Figure 188

The key of C major, for example, then became a tonal complex that, at least in the imagination of theorists, consisted of seven principal tones and five auxiliary alternates. To make matters more confusing, the five auxiliary tones, at least on paper, looked like alterations of the seven principal tones. Only recently has it become apparent that this was only an accident of notation; the problem stemmed from the attempt to represent twelve different tones with a notation system based upon seven letter-names.

MODULATION, SECONDARY DOMINANTS, AND ALTERED CHORDS

The expansion of the seven-tone scale into the twelve-tone scale took place in music while theorists were still attempting to explain tonality in terms of the seven-tone key. This dilemma gave rise to several theories, which were invented to explain the new tones. While all of the theories are in some ways inadequate, all of them have good points with which the student must be familiar.

The oldest theory to explain the new tones that lay outside the seven-tone scale, and the most important from the historical standpoint, is the one of *modulation*. This theory says, in effect, that, when a new tone is introduced into the music, a new seven-tone scale with a new tonic has been established. This theory works very well, especially in simple cases where the new "tonality" is confirmed by a strong cadence. Modulation may then be defined as the process of changing the key or tonic; three types of modulation can be conveniently catagorized: *common chord, chromatic,* and *direct.*

Common Chord Modulation

Figure 189. J. S. Bach, Chorale no. 140, "In allen meinen Taten"

A common chord modulation is one in which a *pivot chord,* common to both keys, is used as the means of leaving the old key and as the entry into the new key. In the above example, the seven-tone scale of C major is established by the first phrase, which then ends in a half cadence on the dominant (V) ; this chord then becomes the tonic (I) of the new seven-tone scale of G major. In other words, the explanation for the new tone, F sharp, is that a new seven-tone scale, to which it belongs, has been established.

Chromatic Modulation

Figure 190. J. S. Bach, Chorale no. 7, "Nun lob', mein Seel', den Herren"

A chromatic modulation dispenses with the common chord and utilizes a chromatic inflection to enter the new key. The student must clearly differentiate here between a chromatic half step (which means the same letter name with a different accidental), and a diatonic half step (which means two different letter names, whether an accidental occurs or not).

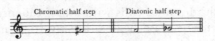

Figure 191

Chorale no. 7 is in the key of A major, the second phrase ending with a full cadence on the tonic. The next phrase begins in A and, at the asterisk, modulates to F sharp minor, the tenor voice moving chromatically, E, E sharp, F sharp. This modulation is then confirmed by an authentic cadence in F sharp minor. The modulation is also considered a chromatic one, even in those cases where the chromatic inflection takes place in a different voice. For example:

Figure 192. J. S. Bach, Chorale no. 74, "O Haupt voll Blut und Wunden"

The first phrase ends in F major, with the C in the tenor voice; the A major chord that begins the next phrase contains the chromatic inflection (C sharp) in the bass voice. This cross relation is somewhat softened by the separation between the two phrases. This example might also be considered as the following:

Direct Modulation

Figure 193. Bach, Chorale no. 74

A direct modulation takes place at the beginning of a new phrase by commencing directly in the new key. In the given example, the third phrase ends with a half cadence in the key of G minor; the new phrase begins directly in C major with the dominant six-five chord, and this, as in the previous example, also produces a cross relation.

The theory of modulation works less well in those cases where there is no strong confirmation of the new tonic. Frequently new notes outside the original seven-tone scale will be introduced into the music, but no new tonal center will be evident, or several different keys will be passed through quickly. In these cases the theory of modulation, in the sense of a new tonality which is firmly established, seems to be a weak explanation for the introduction of the new notes. To explain some of these "transient modulations," the theory of secondary dominants was put forward.

Secondary Dominants. This theory says that any one of the consonant triads in a major or minor key may be preceded by its own V, V⁷, VII, or VII⁷ chord, without producing a modulation. These secondary, or applied, dominants in effect embellish, or intensify, the following chord without really changing its function in the original key.

Figure 194. J. S. Bach, Chorale no. 89, "O Haupt voll Blut und Wunden"

In the key of D major, the dominant chord in the cadence is preceded by its own dominant seventh chord. That is, the sonority is like the dominant seventh chord, as it would be in the key of A major; however, the A major chord does not have the function of I, but still functions as V in the original key.

The process can be extended back for several chords.

Figure 195. J. S. Bach, Chorale no. 279, "Ach Gott und Herr"

The theory of secondary dominants is effective in explaining altered notes when these occur in the "dominant of the dominant" relationship; however, other altered tones do not fit this theory, and so these tones require some other explanation.

Altered Chords

Figure 196. J. S. Bach, Chorale no. 322, "Wenn mein Stündlein vorhanden ist"

The third chord in the example above has the sonority of a "dominant seventh," but the key, of which it would be V, F, is not in the scale of G major. Hence, a more inclusive theory of altered chords has evolved to explain this and other possible alterations.

The B flat, in the bass of the above example, is a chromatic passing tone, altered to increase its drive down to A. It is absorbed into the chord that sounds above it, as the seventh, but the alteration in no way changes the function of the chord in the key; it is still a subdominant seventh chord in G major.

The theory of chromatic alteration goes back to the contrapuntal period, when the concept of *musica ficta* allowed the substitution of the raised leading tone for the seventh scale degree in modes in which that degree was a whole step below the tonic. The inverse of the leading tone principle may be found as far back as plainchant, in which the note B was frequently made B flat as a close upper neighbor to A.

Figure 197

The melodic pull, or tendency to resolve, of the altered note was intensified in the direction of the alteration. In later harmonic periods, this became a basic structural principle, where lines were bent in the direction of their goals.

The theory of alteration operates by producing chords of different color, or sonority, upon roots that still maintain their basic function in a key. Tonal unity is maintained by the root movement, while some variety is afforded by the difference in chord quality. However, it must be emphasized that this theory stems from a contrapuntal phenomenon and not a harmonic one, that is, the choice of the individual tone is for a melodic reason, and only rarely is the individual tone chosen for reasons of harmonic sonority.

There are a number of Bach chorales that illustrate this principle of alteration; indeed, there are a number of chorales that utilize all twelve chromatic pitches in the span of a few phrases

(Numbers 3, 21, 89, and 94, to mention a few). But the following example, although it uses only ten of the possible twelve pitches, shows a clear example of an altered chord and also shows an example of modulation and the use of secondary dominants.

Figure 198. J. S. Bach, Chorale no. 6, "Christus, der ist mein Leben"

This is in the key of F major, but also utilizes the tones B natural, E flat, and D flat. At (*1*), the chromatic passing tone, E flat, makes a V⁷ of IV; at (*2*), the B natural is part of V⁷ of V; the phrase then modulates to the key of the dominant; at (*4*), the D flat is used to pull the tenor line back to C.

At first, when the image of the seven-tone scale was strong, one could properly speak of these as altered tones, that is, one recognized the normal scale degree and was conscious of its being chromatically altered. *Chroma* means color; these alterations were in the nature of color changes that did not radically affect the chord functions within the key. At some point, however, in the evolution of the twelve-tone scale, the alterations became so numerous that the original concept of the seven-tone scale was no longer discernible. At that point the concept of tonality should have changed from that of a seven-tone scale to one of a multi-tone scale. However, our system of notation, based on seven letter names, made it very difficult to accept the twelve-tone chromatic scale as a tonal reality.

In the early years of the twentieth century, the German theorist Heinrich Schenker, realizing that compositions from the classic and romantic periods were elaborations and prolongations of a single tonic triad, suggested that the theory of modulation was no longer valid. He believed that there was only one basic tonality for any composition and that, instead of using the term *modulation*—which implies changing the key—we should say that certain tones within the basic key were intensified by their close adjacent tones. This seems to be a matter of terminology; however, Schenker's basic point is clear. If our conception of tonality is not limited by the concept of the seven-tone scale, then we are under no obligation to explain other tones as belonging to other "keys"; rather, we are obliged to explain how all tones function within the single, unified concept of tonality.

ASSIGNMENTS

A. Analyze Bach Chorale no. 1.
   1. Determine the basic key by the key signature and the first and last phrases.
   2. How many different tones are used in this chorale?
   3. If there are more than seven tones, how would you explain the the notes outside the key signature?
B. Analyze the first three phrases of Bach Chorale no. 138.
   1. Determine the basic key by the key signature and the first and last phrases.
   2. What form (s) of the minor scale occurs in the first three phrases?
   3. What other tones occur and what is your explanation of them?
C. Analyze Bach Chorale no. 270.
   1. This chorale melody is in a mode rather than a major or minor key. Considering only the melody in the soprano part, what is the mode?
   2. Considering the six cadences, what major or minor key is most strongly suggested?
   3. What is your feeling about the last chord?

Chapter 8

Melody Writing

The irreducible minimum of the creative process in music is *melodic invention*. All of the other skills taught to music students —harmony, counterpoint, orchestration, and so on—suppose the preexistence of some melodic germ as a starting point; we harmonize a melody, or we write a counterpoint to a melody, or we orchestrate it. It is important to discuss how melodies are organized structurally—that is, the aspects of form—and for the student to construct some melodies of his own.

Melody may be defined as pitches presented in some orderly arrangement in time; that is, melody, in the general sense, includes the concepts both of pitch and of rhythm as applied to a single line or voice.

The principles of melodic form are best shown by a study of vocal melodies. The history of Western music shows that for several centuries it was concerned almost exclusively with melodies for the human voice. Even after the baroque period, which saw the rise in importance of instrumental music, the *bel canto* vocal melody still remained as an ideal. The idiomatic writing for instruments added such things as arpeggios, scale passages, and extended ranges, but the formal, structural principles for the most part remained unchanged.

Vocal melodies, despite the stylistic varieties of different periods, have three common characteristics, which reflect the limitations of the human voice: they have a limited compass, or range; the motion is more conjunct than disjunct (more steps than skips) ; and they are constructed in short sections. Also, as vocal melodies, they utilize a text, the words and ideas of which are also form determining. These forms are often called *strophic* forms, since they are made in sections like the strophes, or lines, of a poem.

SMALL STROPHIC FORMS

It is apparent that the names given to small forms and segments of music are somewhat analogous to the terms used for sentence construction.

A. Motive (motif, figure) — The smallest melodic germ, made of a few tones and rhythms

B. Phrase member — A part of a phrase made up of motives

C. Phrase — A complete (but not necessarily finished) musical idea, ending with a cadence (regularly four, or sometimes two, measures long)

D. Period — Two related phrases, ending with a strong cadence; analogous to a sentence (regularly eight measures)

E. Double period — Two related periods (regularly sixteen measures)

F. Phrase group — Three or more related phrases

The clearest illustrations of these small forms come from folk songs, children's songs, hymns, and so on. For example, the traditional song "Yankee Doodle" is a period, made up of two similar phrases, each of which can be divided into phrase members.

Figure 199. "Yankee Doodle" (American folk song)

The Brahms Waltz in A flat is an example of the period form from instrumental literature.

Figure 200. Brahms, Waltz in A flat

Two related periods, each of which is made of two related phrases, make a *double period*. Notice that in the English folk song "Greensleeves" the two phrases that make up each period begin alike, but cadence differently.

Figure 201. "Greensleeves" (English carol)

There is not complete agreement on all of these terms—some theorists use the term *sentence* instead of period, and *period* in lieu of double period—but the general idea is clear: larger sections can be divided and subdivided until one discovers the germ motives out of which the music is made. Conversely, we may begin with small motives and arrive at phrases, periods, or double-periods.

It would be a mistake to imply that this additive construction in harmonic or homophonic music stops with the double period or phrase group; periods, double periods, and so on, may become parts or sections of longer works.

SYMMETRY AND BALANCE

As a normal practice, we find that all of these small divisions—motive, phrase member, phrase, or period—occur in pairs. There seems to be some aesthetic necessity to balance a statement with a counterstatement. Theorists have invented terms such as *question* and *answer* to express this need for balance, but the terms probably most commonly used are *antecedent* and *consequent*. The antecedent phrase makes a statement that is answered by the consequent phrase (that is, something that follows the initial idea "in consequence"). The German-American theorist Percy Goetschius, in the last years of the nineteenth century, suggested self-explanatory terms to describe the relationship between such antecedent and consequent pairs; the pairs of phrases or periods were said to be in *parallel, opposite,* or *contrasting* construction. These distinctions are more academic than real, as the student will discover if he seeks examples from his own experience. Probably the most common type of relationship is one of contrasting construction, since *consequent,* by definition, means something different from *antecedent*. Phrases that have contrasting beginnings are apt to end similarly, while phrases with parallel beginnings will have different cadential material. Phrases in opposite construction, where the antecedent is mirrored, or inverted, are likely to be rarest of all.

METRIC STRUCTURE

Phrases may begin and end on either accented or unaccented beats or parts of beats. Some theorists describe those beginnings and endings which are accented as *masculine,* those which are unaccented as *feminine*. The unaccented notes at the beginning of a phrase are called the *anacrusis,* or "pickup" notes.

We may illustrate the various metric possibilities for the beginnings and endings of a four-measure phrase in simple, duple time as follows.

Beginnings may be:

Accented—beginning on a strong beat.

Figure 202

Unaccented (anacrusic) —beginning on a weak beat.

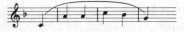

Figure 203

Endings may be:

Accented—ending on a strong beat.

Figure 204

Unaccented—ending on a weak beat.

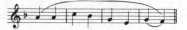

Figure 205

Either type of beginning may be combined with either type of ending, and the metric accents may be broken up rhythmically into any note values. However, the phrase that begins with an anacrusis is perhaps the most natural, since from the world of physical experience we know that one must lift the hammer before striking a blow. The most common ending is the masculine type, where the last note of the phrase falls on an accent.

MELODIC CADENCES

Early monophonic vocal music used closing sections that brought the melody to a point of rest, usually from above. From these we developed patterns of conclusion, called *cadences* (Latin, *cadere;* to fall). The modern term *cadence* usually refers to the harmonic, rather than the purely melodic, dimension of a phrase; the types of harmonic cadence are discussed and systematized in Chapter 11, and the student must refer to this for the definitions of the different cadence names.

The Final Cadence. Almost without exception, the concluding phrase of a melody seeks the tonic note as the final point of rest. This is called a *perfect authentic,* or *full,* cadence. The final note is approached melodically in one of four ways: by step from above, by step from below, by the skip of a fifth down, or by the skip of a fourth up. As we saw earlier, the stepwise approach to the tonic utilized the strongest melodic interval, the second, while the fifth and fourth were the strongest harmonic skips. Here are the concluding phrases from four familiar hymns:

1. Luther, "A Mighty Fortress Is Our God"

2. Crueger, "Now Thank We All Our God"

3. Willis, "It Came upon the Midnight Clear"

4. "Bring a Torch, Jeannette, Isabella" (French carol)

Figure 206

Rarely, the tonic note is approached from above by a skip of a third. This usually means that the next to the last note is a nonharmonic tone (an escape tone), or that the melody is of modal origin.

Figure 207

Figure 208. "O Sacred Head" (Phrygian melody)

Only occasionally will the final tone of a melody be some other member of the tonic chord; this is called an *imperfect authentic* cadence. The last phrase of "The First Noël" ends on the third of the tonic chord.

Figure 209. "The First Noël" (traditional)

The Phrygian chorale "O Sacred Head" (quoted above) was harmonized by Bach in the eighteenth century in a major or a minor key, rather than in a mode. When the key was major the melody ended on the third of the tonic chord.

Figure 210. "O Sacred Head"

All the examples of final cadences given so far have ended normally upon an accented beat, usually the first beat of the measure. There are a few examples where the last note is preceded by an appoggiatura (see Chapter 12), that falls on the accent. This makes a feminine ending for the phrase, with the last melody note occurring on an unaccented beat. However, in most of these cases the chord change still occurs on the accent. A clear example is the German song "O Tannenbaum."

Figure 211. "O Tannenbaum" (German carol)

We may conclude from these examples that the final phrase of the melodies that the student will write will come to rest on the tonic note, usually approached by step from above or below.

Interior Cadences. Cadences that occur in the course of a melody need not imply the same finality that is desirable at the end. Interior phrases, then, will show different degrees of finality, depending upon the composer's intent.

The purpose of the interior cadence is to afford a temporary pause at the end of a musical phrase; this helps define the material in the same way that punctuation does in sentence construction. We may systematize the degrees of finality as follows (the cadence names may be found in Chapter 11) .

Arranged, approximately, in descending order from most to least complete, an interior cadence may be:

    a. Perfect authentic (full) cadence in the tonic key

    b. Same—in a key other than the tonic

    c. Imperfect authentic cadence in the tonic key

    d. Same—in a key other than the tonic

    e. Deceptive cadence in the tonic key

    f. Same—in a key other than the tonic

    g. Half cadence in the tonic key

    h. Same—in a key other than the tonic

This table may be summed up by saying that in the perfect authentic, imperfect authentic, and deceptive cadences the melody will stop on a note of the tonic chord—that is, on scale degrees 1, 3, 5, or 8; for the half cadence, the melody note is usually a member of the dominant or subdominant chords—that is, scale degrees 5, 7, 2, 4, or 6.

Here are some illustrations of the formal points just discussed. Let us suppose that, first, we invent the following rhythmic-metric schematic for a period; the first phrase will use one of the interior cadences from the above table, while the last phrase will be a final cadence.

Figure 212

The melodic beginnings and endings might then be any of these possibilities:

Figure 213

Since this is not a course in composition, we will not emphasize the details of melodic invention. It will be sufficient for the student to do the asssigned tasks at the end of this chapter, approaching these systematically and trusting his intuition. Good melodies are economical. Rather than presenting the listener with a continuous flow of new material, the best melodies, generally, will present a single idea, which is then reused and varied.

EXTENSIONS AND IRREGULARITIES

The regular four-measure phrase is the norm for most melodies, either vocal or instrumental, but occasionally, to avoid monotony, a shorter or longer phrase may be used.

Close examination of a five- or six-measure phrase will often reveal that it is a regular four-measure phrase that has been extended by the repetition, or sequence, of one of its figures, or phrase members. For example:

Figure 214

Such an extension takes place in the course of the phrase; the phrase may also be extended at the end by a small *codetta* that reaffirms the final cadence.

Figure 215

Regular phrases may also be shortened by omitting an expected motive or phrase member.

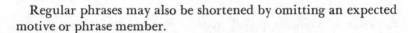

Figure 216

Since the purpose of such abbreviations and extensions is to avoid the constant use of exact symmetry, they occur less frequently than the regular phrase lengths.

ASSIGNMENTS

A. 1. Construct a single four-measure phrase in a major key, ending with a perfect authentic cadence.
   2. Construct a single four-measure phrase in a minor key, ending with a perfect authentic cadence.
B. Construct suitable consequent phrases to follow the given antecedent phrases:

Figure 217

C. 1. In a major key, construct a period of two related four-measure phrases, the first phrase to end with an imperfect authentic cadence, the second phrase with a final cadence.

    2. In a minor key, construct a period of two related four-measure phrases, the first phrase to end with a half cadence, the second phrase with a final cadence.

D. Using the periods constructed in C1 and C2, above:

    1. In the first period, extend one of the phrases by the sequence or repetition of a motive or phrase member.

    2. In the second period, abbreviate one of the phrases by omitting or shortening a motive or phrase member.

E. Construct a double period, sixteen measures long, the key and cadence patterns to be freely chosen.

Chapter 9

Four-Part Vocal Texture (SATB)

The earliest instruction in music composition was undoubtedly contrapuntal in nature. However, in the baroque period, with the shift of emphasis to vertical harmonic combinations, musicians began to study harmonic progressions in which several parts, or lines, were carried forward simultaneously. Probably the earliest harmonic study was concerned with realizing the continuo part on a keyboard instrument. This involved the improvising or the writing out in keyboard texture of a figured bass part (also called *thorough bass*). The student will find some discussion and practical exercises for this type of writing in Chapter 16. From this it became apparent that the progress of each individual line, or voice, in the music could not be easily followed in the multivoiced chords of a clavier part. So, at least from the eighteenth century, the traditional format for the study of harmony has been the four-voice texture of the vocal quartet, using soprano, alto, tenor, and bass parts.

At first the parts were written in *open score,* that is, with each voice on a separate staff and, frequently, in four different clefs. Today we compromise and write the four-voice (SATB) texture on two staves, using the treble and bass clefs. This affords the student the best opportunity to see both the harmonic progression in chords and the conduct of each individual voice. Later, in the study of instrumental music, the student will see how the principles of four-voice harmonic writing are applied to keyboard or ensemble textures.

VOICE RANGES

The compass of each individual human voice is small, approximately an octave and a half in range. The four voices—soprano, alto, tenor, and bass—will use the ranges given below; the soprano and alto parts are written in the treble clef, the tenor and bass parts in the bass clef. Each line has its own note stems; the stems for the soprano and tenor go up, the stems for the alto and bass go down.

Figure 218

These ranges should generally be adhered to; exceptionally, the range of a voice may be increased slightly when this is necessary to complete a melodic line.

DOUBLING

Since the basic harmonic materials are triadic, and the writing is for four voices, there will always be a tone that is *doubled,* that is, the same chord member—root, third, or fifth—will appear in more than one voice, either in the same or in a different octave.

Figure 219

At various times, usually for contrapuntal reasons, any tone in a chord may be doubled. Different theorists have different views on doubling; harmony textbooks usually give the student rules like the following:

A. In a root-position major triad: double, in order of preference, the root, the fifth, the third.

B. In a root-position minor triad: double, in order of preference, the root, the third, the fifth.

Some other texts say that the best notes to double are those of the primary scale degrees (I, IV, and V), whatever the chord type or triad member. This leads to substantially the same result as the above rules.

Figure 220

One can also say that the best tones to double are the least active ones in a key. This means that strongly active tones, those tones which seek resolution to other tones, are the poorest tones to double. For this reason, the leading tone, and the seventh of a seventh chord, are practically never doubled.

In the harmony exercises that follow, the student *will always double the root* of a root-position triad, until he is told otherwise. This eliminates needless speculation in the beginning; in Chapter 10 specific cases of other doublings, usually for reasons of voice leading, will be given.

Obviously, in a succession of root position chords with the roots doubled the doubling must not continue in the *same* two parts, or parallel octaves will result (see Prohibitions in Four-Part writing, below).

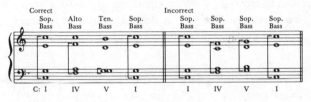

Figure 221

SPACING, DISTANCE, MOTION, AND CROSSING OF PARTS

The kind of spacing that is exhibited by the overtone series, large intervals near the bottom and small intervals near the top of a chord, gives the best resonance for triadic harmony. In order to control the spacing of the upper three parts, two terms are used: *close position* indicates that the upper three voices have each adjacent chord member, with none skipped over; *open position* means that some chord member has been omitted between the soprano and alto, or the alto and tenor, voices.

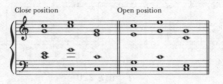

Figure 222

There should be no more than an octave distance between any two adjacent upper voices, that is, between the soprano and alto and between the alto and the tenor. There may be any distance between the tenor and bass voices.

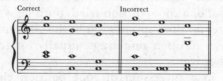

Figure 223

Motion between two or more parts is described as *similar, contrary,* or *oblique.* As a general premise, the individuality of the two parts is best kept by using contrary or oblique motion; however, there are many times when similar motion is desirable.

Figure 224

In four-part writing, it is often desirable to have the bass move contrary to the melody or the upper parts; rarely will all four voices move in the same direction. The one common exception, where all parts move in similar motion, is given below:

Figure 225

In harmonic writing the crossing of parts should be avoided. During the earlier contrapuntal periods, the crossing of voices was common, since this aided in maintaining the individuality of the separate parts. Bach occasionally used crossed parts, particularly in the vocal chorales, but this leads to unnecessary complications that the student is not equipped to handle in the beginning.

The overlapping of adjacent parts is also forbidden, except in the case given below:

Figure 226

CHORD INVERSIONS

When a chord member other than the root is in the bass, the chord is said to be *inverted*. The first inversion of a triad has the chord third in the bass; the second inversion has the chord fifth

in the bass. In the case of seventh chords, which have four different tones, there is also a third inversion.

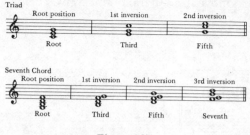

Figure 227

The rules just given governing doubling, spacing, and so on,
for root-position triads also apply to inversions. The figured bass
indication (see Chapter 5, "Symbolization") for each of the inversions is:

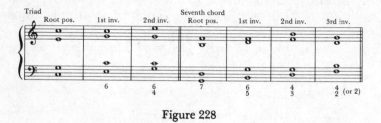

Figure 228

PROHIBITIONS IN FOUR-PART WRITING

The rules governing voice leading that the student will find in
the next chapter are all presented from a positive point of view,
that is, they tell the student what to do. However, it is also useful
to enumerate some things that are prohibited, or at least to be
avoided:

1. In four-part vocal texture each voice should maintain its
individuality. To have two voices do the same thing disturbs the
balance and normal tension between parts. No two voices should
move in consecutive unisons, octaves, or fifths (perfect con-
sonances).

Figure 229

2. Active melodic tones, such as the leading tone, the seventh of a seventh chord, or a chromatically altered tone, should **not** be doubled.

Figure 230

3. Individual voices should not skip such awkward intervals as the augmented second and the augmented fourth. The inversions of these intervals are usable when the active tone resolves properly.

Figure 231

In general, large skips like the seventh and ninth are to be avoided unless they occur in the outer parts and are followed by a change of direction.

Figure 232

Inner parts should normally move as smoothly as possible, that is, keep common tones and move by step or by small skips.

4. The interval of the perfect fourth with the bass voice is to be considered a dissonance; for this reason the second inversion of a triad is considered to be a dissonant chord and should not be left by skip (see under triads in second inversion, p. 132). The fourth between the upper voices is acceptable.

Figure 233

5. As a general premise, in tonal music *dissonance requires resolution to a consonance.* While the student will not encounter this problem until he studies nonharmonic tones or seventh chords, he should be aware that the tonal style requires that dissonant elements be led *stepwise* to an essential consonant tone.

In summary, the essential points covered in this chapter may be briefly stated:

1. Harmony exercises are written for soprano, alto, tenor, and bass voices arranged in pairs on two staves, using the treble and bass clefs.
2. The ranges of these voices are:

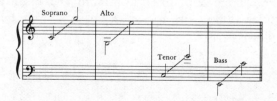

Figure 234

3. In a root-position triad, the root is always doubled unless there is a specific direction otherwise.
4. In close position there is less than an octave space between the soprano and tenor; in open position the space between the soprano and tenor is an octave or greater.
5. Between any two adjacent upper voices there should be no greater distance than an octave; the bass may be any distance below the tenor.
6. Between two voices, or between the bass and the upper parts, contrary and oblique motion are generally preferred to similar motion.
7. Crossed parts are prohibited; parts may overlap only one letter name.
8. Inversions for triads:

Name	Bass Note	Figures
Root position	Root	$\begin{smallmatrix}5\\3\end{smallmatrix}$
1st inversion	Third	6
2nd inversion	Fifth	$\begin{smallmatrix}6\\4\end{smallmatrix}$

Inversions for seventh chords:

Name	Bass Note	Figures
Root position	Root	7
1st inversion	Third	$\begin{smallmatrix}6\\5\end{smallmatrix}$
2nd inversion	Fifth	$\begin{smallmatrix}4\\3\end{smallmatrix}$
3rd inversion	Seventh	$\begin{smallmatrix}4\\2\end{smallmatrix}$ (2)

9. Consecutive unisons, octaves, or fifths are forbidden between any two moving voices.
10. Active melodic tones should not be doubled.
11. Melodic skips of the augmented second and the augmented fourth are forbidden.
12. Inner voices should move smoothly, using common tones, stepwise motion or small skips.
13. The second inversion of a chord is not left by skip.
14. Dissonant tones must resolve, by step, to essential consonant tones.

ASSIGNMENTS

A. Indicate whether the following statements are true or false:
  1. Harmony exercises are written for soprano, alto, tenor, and bass voices on four different staves.
  2. There should be no more than an octave distance between any two adjacent upper parts.
  3. The distance between the bass and tenor voices is immaterial.
  4. In a root-position triad, the root is always doubled, unless there is a specific direction otherwise.
  5. Similar motion is generally preferable to contrary or oblique motion.
B. On manuscript paper, show the ranges for the soprano, alto, tenor, and bass voices.
C. Answer the following questions:
  1. Under what circumstances may two voices overlap?
  2. Under what circumstances may two voices cross?
  3. What is the figured-bass indication for a triad in first inversion?
  4. What is the figured-bass indication for a seventh chord in first inversion?
D. Find the mistakes in the following examples. (There may be more than one mistake in each example) :

Figure 235

Chapter 10

Chord Connection

Traditionally, the study of harmony has been based upon a study of eighteenth-century music (particularly that of Bach) since this was the time when the stylistic features of the harmonic idiom became firmly codified. The harmonic practices of the nineteenth and early twentieth centuries extend and develop the vocabulary of this harmonic style, but the basic principles can best be seen in such eighteenth-century music as the Bach chorales.[1]

The method followed here will be to show the student the part writing principles that can be discovered by analysis of eighteenth-century music, but without emphasizing baroque stylistic details. This provides a foundation for examining nineteenth-century harmonic developments, and these, in turn, provide a route to the music of our own time.[2]

There are two basic problems with which the student of harmony must first contend: *chord choice,* or how one chooses the chords to harmonize a melody, and *chord connection,* or the acceptable ways of progressing from one chord to another. Many harmony books have the student cope with both problems simultaneously; however, for the sake of clarity, in the beginning we will examine the problems separately. Later, of course, after one has acquired some experience, both things must be handled

[1] The student should purchase one of the modern editions of the *371 Chorales* by J. S. Bach for analysis and study. A few selected chorales for classroom analysis will be found in Appendix 4 at the end of this volume.

[2] The approach followed here, though different in many significant details, is largely based upon that of A. I. McHose in his important treatise *The Contrapuntal Harmonic Technique of the 18th Century* (New York: Appleton-Century-Crofts, 1947).

together. Since the more difficult of the problems, requiring considerable musicianship, is chord choice, we will defer that until the conventions of part writing have been thoroughly explored.

Types of harmonic progression can be reduced to four situations, depending upon the distance that the roots of the chords move. The four situations are: (1) repeated chords, where the root remains the same; (2) chords a fifth apart, where the root moves up or down a fifth (or its inversion, a fourth); (3)· chords a second apart, where the root moves up or down a second (or a seventh); and (4) chords a third apart, where the root moves up or down a third (or a sixth). For example, while there is a great difference, musically, between the progression I IV and II VI, there is no difference in the voice leading, since the roots of each pair move the same distance.

C: I   IV   II   VI

Figure 236

One must acquire some technical facility in connecting such pairs of chords before attempting the harmonization of a melody. For the exercises at the end of this chapter, the problem of chord choice is eliminated by giving both the melody and the bass; the student achieves practice in part writing by filling in the inner parts according to the given rules.

PRINCIPLES OF PART WRITING—TRIADS IN ROOT POSITION

The following rules are predicated upon two conditions:
1. They deal with consonant (that is, major and minor) triads in root position.
2. Unless specifically excepted, each triad is complete, with the root doubled.

Repeated Triads

1. When a triad is repeated, one may *retain* the same open or close position in the second chord.

Figure 237

2. When a triad is repeated, one may *change* from open to close position, or vice versa.

Figure 238

Which of the two possibilities is chosen depends upon the melody and the desired position of the second chord for what follows. The student should note that when a chord is repeated with a different soprano note, if the chord position (open or close) is maintained, the three upper parts will move in similar motion; if the chord position is changed (from open to close, or vice versa), the three upper parts will show contrary and oblique motion.

3. *Exception: Repeated triads with a chromatic inflection.* A triad may be repeated with a chromatically altered third, that is, it may change from a major to a minor triad, or vice versa. This requires no new rule; the two principles given above apply exactly, with the addition of the chromatic inflection.

a. This is more common between two different phrases than in the course of one phrase.

b. The chromatically altered third is found more often in the same voice than in a different voice. When the chromatic inflection takes place in a different voice, this is called *cross-relation* (or *false relation*).

Figure 239

Triads a Fifth Apart

1. When the root moves up or down a fifth (or a fourth), keep the common tone in the same voice and move the other two voices by step to the nearest chord tones.

Figure 240

2. When the root moves up or down a fifth (or a fourth), do not keep the common tone in the same voice but move the three upper parts in similar motion.

Figure 241

A variation of the first two principles sometimes occurs when it is desirable for the leading tone to ascend to the tonic. While this may occur in the course of a phrase, it is most common in the final cadence when the melody moves 2–1.

3. When the root moves up or down a fifth (or fourth), the third and fifth of the first chord go to the root of the second; the fifth in the second chord is omitted, and the root is tripled.

Figure 242

4. When the root moves up or down a fifth (or fourth), the third of the first chord skips to the third of the second chord; keep the common tone and move the remaining voice by step.

Figure 243

Triads a Second Apart

1. When the root moves up or down a second, move the three upper parts contrary to the bass, to the nearest chord tones.

Figure 244

The above rule is the most frequent procedure when the root moves up or down a major or minor second; however, there are two situations that require modifications of this. In the progression V#3–VI in a minor key, the use of the above rule would result in a melodic skip of an augmented second in some voice. Therefore, for the progression V#3–VI in minor, the following rule must be used; it also may be used for V–VI in major, and for some other progressions, where the root moves up a second.

2. When the root moves up a second, move one upper part in parallel thirds with the bass; move the two remaining voices to the nearest chord tones, contrary to the bass. This will result in a doubled third in the second chord.

Figure 245

If this second procedure were followed in the progression IV–V, a doubled leading tone would result:

Figure 246

Since the doubling of this active tone is undesirable, another procedure must be used.

3. When the root moves up or down a second, move one upper part in parallel thirds with the bass; the two remaining voices, moving contrary to the bass, will both *skip* to chord tones.

Figure 247

The skip of a third in one of the voices is often filled in with a passing tone.

Triads a Third Apart

1. When the root moves up or down a third (or a sixth), keep the *two* common tones in the same voice and move the other voice by step to the nearest chord tone.

Figure 248

This is the usual procedure for two chords a third apart; however, because of a given soprano movement or for other reasons of part writing, it is necesssary to have an alternative procedure.

2. When the root moves up or down a third (or a sixth), double the third of the second chord; this may result in the retention of two common tones, one common tone, or no common tones.

Figure 249

A word of caution is necessary here; most of the above procedures, if followed correctly, make it virtually impossible to write consecutive fifths or octaves. It is possible, though, to follow the last procedure and produce consecutive fifths.

Figure 250

Both of these cases are unacceptable and must be rejected.

3. *Exception: Triads a third apart with chromatic inflection (chromatic third-relation)*. When the root moves up or down a major or minor third, a chromatic inflection may take place in one of the voices. This requires no new rule; the first principle given above (retaining two common tones, that is, letter names) applies exactly, with the addition of the chromatic inflection.

    a. This is more common in the eighteenth century between two different phrases than in the course of one phrase. However, in the nineteenth century the chromatic third-relation is common in the course of a phrase.

    b. The chromatically altered letter name is usually kept in the same voice; when it takes place in a different voice, a cross relation occurs.

    c. Characteristically, the quality (major or minor) of both chords is the same.

Chromatic third-relation (major triads) :

Figure 251

Chromatic third-relation (minor triads) :

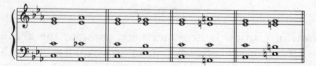

Figure 252

Cross relation (rare) :

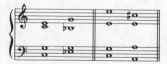

Figure 253

At this point all the part-writing rules have been explained. Now go to the exercises at the end of this chapter (p. 135) for some experience in the practical application of this knowledge. Skill in the handling of the material must be achieved by drill and repetition.

Here are some suggestions to help you solve these exercises:

1. On p. 134, there is a one-page summary of the part-writing rules; keep this in front of you as a reminder while solving the exercises, for as long as this is necessary or until all of the rules have been firmly committed to memory.

2. The exercises are divided into three groups: group 1 uses part-writing rules A1, A2, B1, B2, C1, and D1 (that is, approximately half of the part-writing rules); group II uses all of the part-writing rules for root-position chords; group III uses the rules for chords in inversions.

3. The various rules for each root movement are to be applied pragmatically, in the order given. For example, if you find two chords a fifth apart in an exercise, try the first rule for fifth-related chords—if the rule works, go on to the next chord; if it does not, try the next rule for fifth-related chords, and so on until you find the correct one. Later, you will find some situations where two or three different rules will all work equally well; in these cases you may freely choose the solution you prefer.

Triads in first inversion

The continual use of chords in root position often results in an angular bass part that contains more skips than steps. In order to have, at least part of the time, a more stepwise bass line, chords are sometimes used in inversion. Generally speaking, except at certain key structural points such as the final cadence, chords in first inversion may be freely substituted for root-position chords. The reasons for choosing an inversion rather than a chord in root position will be clearer when we discuss chord choice; for the moment we are concerned with the principles of connection into and out of the first inversion of a chord.

No new part-writing rules are needed for first-inversion chords; the voice leading can be solved by using the right procedure for doubling.

1. When a primary triad (I, IV, or V) is used in first inversion, double, in order of preference: the soprano, the bass, the inner voice.

Which voice receives the double note must be decided on the basis of context; the two inner voices must move as smoothly as possible, retaining common tones and proceeding by steps and small skips. Begin by doubling the soprano note; reject this only if it causes some part-writing defect—for example, consecutive octaves or fifths. If you do have to reject it, double the bass note and, if this is an acceptable solution, go on. If neither the soprano nor the bass doublings work, double the inner voice. Do not double the leading tone or an altered tone.

2. When a secondary triad (II, III, VI, or VII) is used in first inversion, double the third of the triad. In the few cases where this makes the part-writing defective, as a second choice double the root. *Exception: do not double the root of VII, but as second choice, double the fifth.*

Triads in second inversion

While triads in first inversion occur frequently in eighteenth- and nineteenth-century music, the triad in second inversion is comparatively rare. This is because in the second inversion ($^6_4$) one of the voices is a fourth above the bass, and in this period the fourth was considered a dissonant interval. Unlike the first inversion, which may be freely approached or left by skip, the second inversion requires special treatment because of this dissonant element. No new part-writing procedures are necessary for the second inversion; the bass tone, the fifth of the chord, is always doubled.

The most common occurrence of the second inversion triad is as a decoration of a root-position triad on the same bass note. The upper parts may be approached by step, skip, or repeated note; they resolve *downward* by step, while the bass remains. Since this generally occurs on the strong beat at a cadence, it is frequently called the *accented, cadential* six-four chord.

Figure 254

Next in frequency, the *passing* six-four chord occurs *between* two chords, either between the root position and first inversion of the same chord or between two different chords and, characteristically, on the unaccented beat. The bass note is approached and left by step, in the same direction.

Figure 255

The remaining forms of the six-four chord occur less frequently than the cadential or passing forms, and they are more properly explained by nonharmonic activity. In the first two examples below, the upper parts are neighboring or passing tones; the third case results from an arpeggiated bass line.

Figure 256

In all these cases the dissonance must be treated correctly, that is, the dissonant notes are resolved by step to essential chord tones, or the arpeggiated bass continues on to the root or third of the chord. In all forms of the six-four chord, the fifth should always be doubled. In the rare cases where some other doubling occurs, it is usually for reasons of contrapuntal voice leading, and the instances of this are negligible.

Now solve the exercises in group III at the end of this chapter; these illustrate all of the root-position part-writing rules explained above and also contain chords in first and second inversion.

SUMMARY OF PRINCIPLES OF CHORD CONNECTION

Rules for connecting root position, consonant triads, arranged according to root movement			
A. Repeated triads	B. 5th related (5th or 4th, up or down)	C. 2nd related (2nd or 7th, up or down)	D. 3rd related (3rd or 6th, up or down)
1. Retain same position (open or close)	1. Common tone	1. Contrary motion	1. Two common tones
2. Change position (from open to close, or vice versa)	2. Similar motion	2. Parallel 3rds to doubled 3rd in second chord	2. Doubled 3rd in second chord
3. Exception: with chromatic inflection	3. Tripled root, 5th omitted	3. Parallel 3rds, skip	3. Exception: with chromatic inflection
	4. 3rd to 3rd		

The above rules presuppose that each triad is complete, with the root doubled, except where expressly stated otherwise. In leaving a chord with unusual doubling, return at once to the doubled root.

Chords in First Inversion
Part writing is solved by correct doubling:
1. In primary triads (I, IV, and V) double in order of preference:

> Soprano note
> Bass note
> Inner-voice note

2. In secondary triads (II, III, VI, and VII) double the third or root (exception: in VII, double the third or fifth).

Chords in Second Inversion
1. Double the bass tone (fifth).
2. The fourth with the bass must be treated as a dissonance.

EXERCISES

A. Add the inner parts, using the rules for: repeated triads (A1, A2), triads a fifth apart (B1, B2), triads a second apart (C1), and triads a third apart (D1). Complete the Roman numeral analysis as you do the exercise, showing the modulations, if any. Determine the principal key from the key signature and the last bass note. In a common chord modulation, the chord before the chord containing the new tone is usually the common chord.

Figure 257

EXERCISES

B. Add the inner parts, using all of the part-writing rules for root-position triads. In each root-movement category try the first procedure first. If this gives an acceptable solution, go on to the next chord; if it does not, try the next procedure for that root movement. Add the roman numeral analysis.

Figure 258

EXERCISES

C. Add the inner parts, using the rules for root-position triads and for
first and second inversions. When a chord occurs in an inversion,
solve the part writing into the inversion by first solving the doubling.
When going from an inversion back to a root-position triad, return
to the doubled root. When two root-position chords occur, use the
rules based upon root movement.

1. "Jesu, meine Freude" (German chorale)

2. "Wenn wir in höchsten Nöten sein" (German chorale)

3. "Danket dem Herren" (German chorale)

4. "O Haupt voll Blut und Wunden" (German chorale)

5. "Vom Himmel Hoch" (German chorale)

6. "Wer nur den lieben Gott" (German chorale)

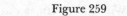

Figure 259

Chapter 11

Chord Choice

Choosing the chords to harmonize a given melody is one of the more difficult but, at the same time, one of the most interesting and creative of all the tasks the harmony student will encounter. After acquiring some skill in chord connection, he must put that technique to some practical musical use: in this case the four-part settings of given melodies. The melodies may be existing traditional ones, or they may be composed by the student; they may be in the style of folk songs, popular songs, hymns, or chorales.

Every tonal melody carries with it certain harmonic implications; it is this—what the French composer-teacher, Vincent d'Indy, called the "true harmony"—that the student must endeavor to discover for every melody. This does not imply that there is only one correct harmony for a melody; it means, rather, that there may be several possible settings, all of which will be compatible with the possibilities and limitations inherent in the given line. It is these implications, which lie hidden in the melody itself, that the composer attempts to unlock and bring to realization by his harmonization. The goal, then, at least in the beginning, should be to discover an appropriate harmonization, rather than the most obscure, extreme, or esoteric one.

The harmonization of any melody begins with a searching analysis of the given material. The melody is divided into *phrases,* or small component parts, and these are examined for their cadential and tonal implications. For example, here are three melodies—a folk song, a strophic hymn, and a chorale tune.

1. "Henry Martin" (English folk song)

2. Croft, "O God Our Help in Ages Past"

3. "Jesu, meine Freude" (German chorale)

Figure 260

Each of these melodies has a text, and each has some of the characteristics that are peculiar to its genre. The folk song has an odd number of phrases, a changing meter, and is in a medieval mode (Dorian); the hymn has four balanced phrases, possibly reflecting the lines of verse, and is in a major key; the German chorale has an odd number of phrases, a strong rhythmic drive interrupted by long holds, and is in a minor key. All of these factors would influence appropriate settings for these melodies; but the melodies have common cadential patterns, and the characteristics and tonal implications of these give the melody its formal punctuation. Analysis of a melody, then, begins by determining what kind of cadential feeling occurs at the ends of its phrases and relating this to a key or tonality.

HARMONIC CADENCES

In Chapter 8 we reviewed the melodic characteristics of the cadence; this linear view now must be coordinated with the harmonic aspect.

Final Cadences. The purpose of the final cadence is to bring the music to a definite conclusion; the feeling of finality must be complete. Only two types of cadence normally occur at the end of tonal compositions: the *authentic* (or *full*), and the *plagal* cadence. These are further qualified by the terms *perfect* and *imperfect.*

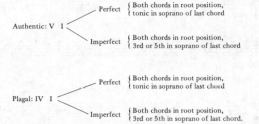

Authentic: V I

    Perfect { Both chords in root position, tonic in soprano of last chord

    Imperfect { Both chords in root position, 3rd or 5th in soprano of last chord

Plagal: IV I

    Perfect { Both chords in root position, tonic in soprano of last chord

    Imperfect { Both chords in root position, 3rd or 5th in soprano of last chord.

Interior Cadences. Cadences that occur in the course of a composition produce different degrees of finality; they may be as final as the concluding cadence, or they may sound less conclusive, implying to the listener that the stop is a temporary one and that the music will continue.

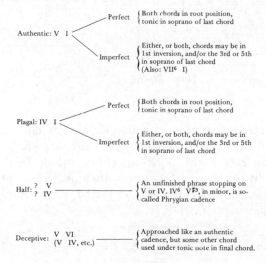

Authentic: V I

    Perfect { Both chords in root position, tonic in soprano of last chord

    Imperfect { Either, or both, chords may be in 1st inversion, and/or the 3rd or 5th in soprano of last chord (Also: VII⁶ I)

Plagal: IV I

    Perfect { Both chords in root position, tonic in soprano of last chord

    Imperfect { Either, or both, chords may be in 1st inversion, and/or the 3rd or 5th in soprano of last chord

Half: ? V / ? IV ——— { An unfinished phrase stopping on V or IV. IV⁶ V♯⁵, in minor, is so-called Phrygian cadence

Deceptive: V VI / (V IV, etc.) ——— { Approached like an authentic cadence, but some other chord used under tonic note in final chord.

For purposes of systematization, analyze the following phrases, identifying the cadences according to key and type:

Figure 261

SELECTING THE CHORDS

Chord selection begins by dividing the given melody into phrases and deciding what type of cadence, in what key, is appropriate for each phrase. The first choice should be the cadence that confirms the strongest, or most obvious, feeling of the line; alternate solutions may then be considered. For example, play or sing the following phrase:

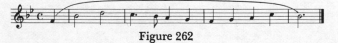

Figure 262

The basic question that one asks, then, is: Does the phrase sound finished or unfinished? In this case the phrase sounds complete, and, therefore, the most obvious choice is a perfect authentic cadence (V I) in the tonic key, B flat. If this were the first phrase of a longer melody and the full stop was not desirable so near the beginning, then the finished effect could be softened by using an imperfect authentic cadence (V I^6), or deceptive cadence (V VI), or even an imperfect authentic cadence (V$^{\#3}$ I) in the related key of G minor.

Determine the last two chords for the following ten phrases. Play the melody through; decide whether it is finished or unfinished; choose the proper cadence; and test this out by playing the last two chords in close position under the last two melody notes. Do not be concerned with part writing at this point. Make an alternative choice for the cadence and test this out by playing the last two chords. Here is a sample phrase:

Imperfect authentic cadence in F major

Half cadence in D minor

Figure 263

Figure 264

After the ending of the phrase has been decided upon, we give our attention next to the beginning of the phrase. A phrase normally begins with either the tonic or dominant chords, or sometimes both. Our sample phrase would begin:

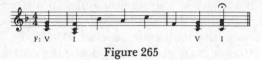

Figure 265

Using the above ten phrases, for which the cadences were determined, write in the key and the first chord, or the first two chords if the phrase begins with an anacrusis. The first phrase might be:

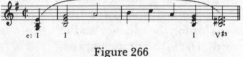

Figure 266

After the ending and the beginning of the phrase have been determined, the chords for the remainder of the phrase are chosen. Theoretically at least, each melody tone may be the root, third, or fifth of a triad; write down the three roman numerals under each tone and, after trial-and-error speculation, circle the best choice. The sample phrase might be harmonized:

Figure 267

Of course, there are always several possible choices, and some may suggest a modulation to another key. Exercise 1 of Figure 264 might suggest these chords:

Figure 268

Do the remainder of the phrases in a similar manner, writing down the three possibilities for each melody note and circling your choice. After the chords are selected, the phrase should be played at the piano. Play the chosen chords in close position below each melody note; do not be concerned about the correctness of the voice leading.

After choosing the chords for these ten phrases, you will probably feel the need for some systematic approach to chord choice. Instead of making subjective decisions based on random trial and error, you need a method to evaluate the various possibilities inherent in the melody. While there is no foolproof way, other than that of experience and talent, theorists have attempted to generalize some basic principles for chord succession.

Rameau, an eighteenth-century contemporary of Bach, thought that the three primary triads (I, IV, V) were the most important chords, and that the diatonic scale could be harmonized using only those triads. It is undoubtedly true that the strength of the eighteenth-century style is due in large part to the great frequency of these primary triads.

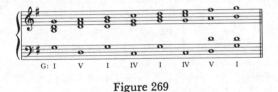

G: I   V   I   IV   I   IV   V   I

Figure 269

Following this reasoning, Goetschius, at the end of the nineteenth century, divided all triads into three classifications: tonic, dominant, and subdominant.[1] The subordinate triads (VI, III, II) belong to these same three classifications, respectively, and are treated as substitutes for the principal chords.

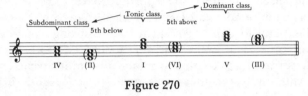

Figure 270

[1] Percy Goetschius, *The Material Used in Musical Composition* (New York: G. Schirmer, 1889), pp. 21, 74, 113.

The leading-tone triad is conspicuous by its absence; it is treated as the incomplete V⁷ in Goetschius's table of discords.[2] He groups discords into four classifications according to their distance from the tonic in ascending fifths.

Figure 271

First-class chords, a fifth higher than I, have the strongest tendency to progress down to the tonic; second-class chords, two fifths above I, have a strong tendency toward first-class chords; third- and fourth-class chords are even more remote, being the third and fourth fifths above the tonic.

In this arrangement, VII is said to be an incomplete V⁷, VII⁷ an incomplete V⁹, IV⁷ is derived from the incomplete II⁹, and so on. The contemporary theorist A. I. McHose uses a somewhat similar chord classification scheme,[3] but he avoids labeling the leading-tone triad as an incomplete V⁷. Piston, on the other hand, follows Goetschius in calling VII⁷ an incomplete V⁹, but instead of using a chord classification scheme, he gives the student a table of common root progressions.[4]

In selecting effective chord progressions, such classification schemes or tables of root movement are of some assistance to the inexperienced student. The charts of Goetschius are based upon two ideas: (1) the substitute subordinate triads have two tones in common with their principal counterparts and (2) the classification of discords is based upon a root movement of falling fifths that, in turn, allows the chord seventh to be resolved by the next lower classification. Since our approach to part writing was on the basis of root movement, rather than chord function, it will be useful to generalize a principle of strong and weak chord progressions, based upon root movement. The following design applies primarily to consonant major and minor triads; however, after you study seventh chords and altered chords, review this

2 Goetschius, p. 74.

3 Allen Irvine McHose, *The Contrapuntal Harmonic Technique of the 18th Century* (New York: Appleton-Century-Crofts, 1947), p. 13–17.

4 Walter Piston, *Harmony* (New York: W. W. Norton, 1962), p. 18.

chart again, since it also applies in certain ways to that material (for example, root movements down a fifth, and up a second, produce the resolution for the seventh of a seventh chord).

ROOT MOVEMENT CHART

Normal, frequent, or strong progressions:	Less common, infrequent, or weak progressions:
1. Down a fifth	1. Up a fifth
2. Up a second (M or m)	2. Down a second (M or m)
3. Down a third (M or m)	3. Up a third (M or m)

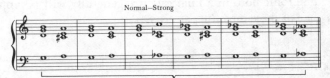

Normal—Strong

2. Up a second (M or m)

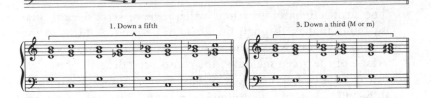

1. Down a fifth   3. Down a third (M or m)

Infrequent—Weak

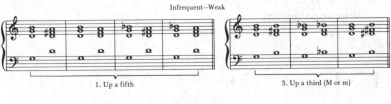

1. Up a fifth   3. Up a third (M or m)

2. Down a second (M or m)

Figure 272

In using this or a similar chart, one must realize that it does not guarantee a successful chord progression, nor is any chord progression absolutely forbidden. The chart shows what kinds of root movement happen most frequently; however, in a particular situation an infrequently used progression may be most effective.

MELODIC CADENCES

Finally, we must review the most common melodic cadences, and show how these are most often harmonized.

The tonic note in a final cadence generally will be approached by one of these melodic patterns:

Figure 273

The strongest harmonizations will progress: second class, first class, tonic; that is, through the circle of descending fifths to the tonic. In the cases where the second-class chord cannot be used (because of the given melody), the chord preceding the first-class chord is usually I, I^6 or I^6_4. The bass line to these progressions will be discussed in the following section. The following approaches should be memorized and transposed to other major and minor keys:

Authentic Cadences

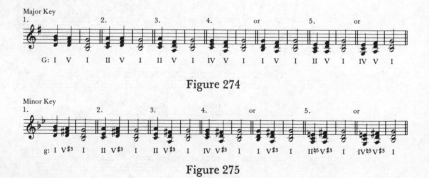

Figure 274

Figure 275

Deceptive Cadences. The same approaches may be transformed into *deceptive cadences* by substituting VI for the final I in each cadence.

Figure 276

Half Cadences. *Half cadences,* which are unfinished, occur when the phrase stops short of the tonic chord; the last chord is most often V, but occasionally it is IV.

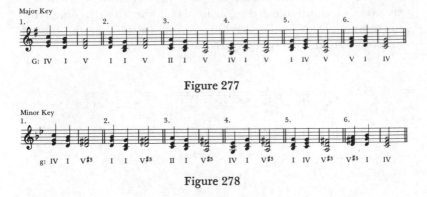

Figure 277

Figure 278

The deceptive and half cadences also should be transposed, and played at the keyboard, in other major and minor keys.

THE BASS LINE

After the chords for the phrase have been chosen, you should write the *bass line*. Later, after considerable experience in choosing the chords and writing the bass part, you may reverse the process or simultaneously write the bass line while choosing the chords. In some cases, the actual line of the bass part will suggest an appropriate choice of chords; in other cases the harmonies will be arrived at first. Ultimately it does not matter which is discovered first, since both are inseparably connected.

The two outer parts, the soprano and bass, are the most important parts of any harmonic texture; they are the parts that are most easily heard and therefore the ones that should be the strongest melodic lines. Inner voices, the alto and tenor, are more likely to be unobtrusive; they frequently keep common tones or move by step or small skips. Since the soprano melody is usually a preexistent given part and therefore not subject to change, it is the bass part that will require the most attention. A good bass line should have both stepwise motion and some skips. The skips are generally necessary at the ends of phrases in order to give strong cadences; much of the beginning and the course of the phrase will be made of conjunct (stepwise) motion. In order to make an interesting line, the bass part cannot be made exclusively of chord roots. For example, if the chords chosen for the sample phrase in the previous section (p. 146) are all placed in root position, we have this bass part:

Figure 279

As a bass line, this contains many skips and could be improved by the use of more stepwise motion. This is the purpose of using chord inversions. Theoretically, each chord could have three different bass notes; in practice, the second inversion is usable only in certain particular situations, for reasons given earlier (see p. 132), but the first inversion can generally be freely substituted for the root position. There are some exceptions, of course: the cadence chords usually are best kept in root position in order to make the cadence more emphatic, and the dissonant, diminished or augmented, secondary triads are usually found only in first inversion.

To illustrate, let us make two chord choices for the sample phrase.

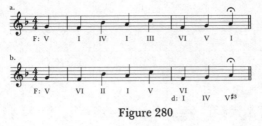

Figure 280

In order to make as good a bass line as possible we will put down all of the choices available by inversions and, in some cases, other octaves. The above two harmonizations then have these possible bass notes:

Figure 281

From these possibilities several different bass lines might be chosen for each of the chord choices. For example, here are two basses for each harmonization:

Figure 282

Each line has some use of both skips and steps, and, in a very general way, the bass has been arranged so that it moves in contrary motion against the soprano.

Now return to the ten melodic phrases given on p. 145; for each phrase make at least two chord selections, and for each chord choice make at least two different bass lines. This will give at least four bass lines for each melodic phrase, from which the best one may then be selected. For the moment, it is not so important to decide that one chord choice or bass line is better than another one; what is important is that you develop the capacity to make several harmonizations and several different basses from which a selection may ultimately be made.

The usual chord choices for the cadences that were given on p. 150 now need to be completed by the addition of the bass parts. In the approach to the authentic cadence, the following basses are the most common (in both major and minor keys):

Figure 283

When these basses are added to the earlier chord choices, some attention then must be given to correct part writing. There are only a few places in the major key where consecutives are a problem, but in the minor key care must be taken to avoid the melodic skip of the augmented second. The common approaches to the authentic, deceptive, and half cadences are given below for the major and minor keys; these must be studied, played at the keyboard, and transposed to other keys.

Figure 284

Figure 285

Figure 286

THE INNER PARTS

After the chords have been chosen for the phrase and the (figured) bass part written, the harmonization is, for all practical purposes, complete. Adding the inner parts should be a routine matter. Treat the melody with figured bass in exactly the same manner as a part writing exercise, using the rules based upon root movement (or the doubling procedures when an inversion occurs). The basic difference between this kind of completion and the earlier exercises is that the chord choice and bass line have been done by the student, rather than by someone else.

Frequently, when adding the inner parts a difficulty in part writing will be discovered that was not apparent when the chord choice was made. In fact, in a few cases you may find that acceptable part writing is literally impossible with a given bass line and chord choice. In those cases where difficulties appear, you should have no hesitation in changing the original chord choice or bass line or both in order to improve the finished harmonization.

After some practice and experience in adding the inner parts, this last step should be done at the keyboard. Using the melody and the figured bass, play the first chord, holding down the keys until the part writing for the next chord is thought out, then play the next chord, and continue in this manner for the remainder of the harmonization.

Complete the given phrases, following the method described above (and outlined below):

1. Determine the key and type of cadence.
2. Write the bass notes for the end and the beginning of the phrase.
3. Choose the remaining chords for the entire phrase.
4. Write a bass line, adding the necessary figures.
5. Add the inner parts.

Figure 287

Chapter 12

Harmonizing a Melody

The exercises in chord choice have so far been limited to the phrase; the process must now be extended to a multiphrase melody. Our examples will continue to be drawn from eighteenth-century chorale-like melodies, although the harmonization procedure is applicable to a variety of other melody types.

ANALYSIS OF THE MELODY

The eighteenth-century chorale melody consisted of several phrases, generally from four to eight, corresponding to the lines of the text. The melodies themselves usually stayed within the confines of the seven-tone key or mode; however, the harmonizations of these melodies by Bach and his contemporaries usually used alterations or modulations. None of the 371 settings of chorale tunes made by Bach stays within a seven-tone scale. Some of them use only a few alterations, as, for instance, secondary dominants to emphasize cadence chords, but most make full-fledged modulations to related keys with strong cadences and sufficient material to establish a new temporary tonic. There are a few cases where Bach chooses to go outside the related key system, but this is neither typical nor necessary.

Following is a four-phrase chorale melody; its analysis should determine (1) the principal tonality (decided by the key signature and the final cadence), (2) the cadence point at the ends of phrases (here indicated by the long note and fermata), and (3) the cadence type and key for each phrase.

Figure 288. "Das neugeborne Kindelein" (German chorale)

It is (1) in the key of G minor, (2) it contains four four-measure phrases, and (3) the cadences are probably the following: phrase 1—half cadence in the tonic key (G minor); phrase 2—perfect authentic cadence in the dominant key (D minor); phrase 3—perfect authentic cadence in the relative major, or mediant key (B flat major); phrase 4—a perfect authentic cadence in the tonic key (G minor).

Bach's harmonization (given below) confirms this plan exactly, with the addition of the Picardy third to the second and fourth cadences.

Figure 289. J. S. Bach, Chorale no. 178, "Das neugeborne Kindelein"

(Since this harmonization uses nonharmonic tones and seventh chords, a detailed discussion is not possible until that material has been presented.)

After working out the cadence formulas, use the procedures developed earlier to complete the harmonization of each phrase, that is, choose the chords to complete the phrase, write a (figured) bass line, and add the inner parts.

HARMONIZING AN UNFIGURED BASS

To better understand the process of harmonization, it is sometimes useful to begin with the bass part rather than the soprano. In composing a melody to a given bass part, the student is often better able to see the contrapuntal relationship that should exist between these most important outer parts.

The technique is similar to that of harmonizing a soprano: begin with an analysis of the line, determining key, modulations, and cadences. (The types of cadence are more easily determined from a bass line than from a melody.) Then select the remaining chords for the phrase, and, from the possible chord tones, choose the soprano melody. When the melody and figured bass are complete, add the inner parts, using the rules with which you are already familiar.

It is also useful to make more than one chord choice, and also to construct different sopranos from each chord selection. You may also first write the soprano line as a counterpoint against the bass and, from this two-voice framework, then determine the chord progression. This will be note-against-note counterpoint, of course, until we have discussed the possibilities of non-harmonic tones.

For example, consider this bass line of four phrases:

Figure 290

The cadences suggested are: phrase 1—a half cadence in E flat major, or an authentic cadence in the dominant key, B flat major; phrase 2—an authentic cadence in G minor; phrase 3—an imperfect authentic cadence in the relative minor, C minor; and phrase 4—a perfect authentic cadence in E flat major.

Within this cadential framework, the following chord progressions might be chosen:

Figure 291

We could then make two soprano lines for each of the chord choices.

Figure 292

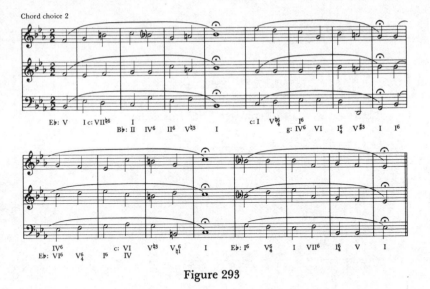

Figure 293

From these possibilities the best soprano could then be chosen and the inner parts added to complete the harmonization.

EXERCISES

Following the procedures just given, harmonize the given soprano and bass parts, using triads in root position, first and second inversion, and modulation to related keys.

1. "Christus, der ist mein Leben" (German chorale)

2. "Ermuntre dich" (German chorale)

3. "Puer natus" (German chorale)

4. "Herzlich tut mich verlangen" (German chorale)

5. "Nun danket alle Gott" (German chorale)

6.

7.

8.

9.

10.

Figure 294

Part III
Elaboration

Chapter 13

Nonharmonic Tones (Melodic Elaboration)

The multivoiced texture of Western music is usually described as either *harmonic* or *contrapuntal,* depending upon whether the vertical or horizontal aspect of the music is being emphasized. When all of the parts or voices move together in time, the effect is largely *harmonic,* or *chordal.* For example, in the closing theme from the last movement of the Pathétique Sonata, all of the parts move in the same general rhythm.

Figure 295. Beethoven, Sonata opus 13

The concept of *counterpoint,* on the other hand, requires that the individuality of the different voice lines be emphasized. Indeed, one might say that the essence of counterpoint is to be found in the contrary motion and different rhythm between two or more parts, since it is chiefly these concepts which keep one line distinct from another. This kind of melodic elaboration uses dissonant nonharmonic tones as well as consonant chord tones.

In one of the subordinate themes from the Pathétique Sonata, while the effect is still largely harmonic, Beethoven manages to keep the two lines distinctly separate. In the first phrase, this is done principally by contrary motion, since the two lines

169

have substantially the same rhythm; in the second phrase, the individuality of the two voices is heightened by having them also move at different times.

Figure 296. Beethoven, Sonata opus 13

In order to coordinate the vertical and horizontal fields in multivoiced music, theorists attempt to determine the prevailing harmonic background of a composition—that is, the basic chord progression—and then describe the deviations from this that occur in the individual horizontal lines. These deviations from the background harmony are called *nonharmonic* (or *nonchord*) tones, since the melodic activity in the individual lines involves tones that are not in the prevailing harmony.

There are no universally accepted definitions of these non-harmonic tones. The two principal schools of thought agree that the criteria for describing the nonharmonic situations are: (1) how the dissonant tone relates spatially to the surrounding chord tones, and (2) where it occurs in terms of metric accent; they disagree as to which of these is to have the primary role in the definition. Most theory books have chosen the former of these two possibilities, since the determination of the metric accent is often difficult to make or is misleading. While there is good agreement about metric accents in eighteenth- and nineteenth-century music, there is less unanimity concerning, for example, fourteenth-century music, where there are no bar lines, or some twentieth-century music, where the bar line is meaningless or is a matter of convenience. For this reason, the definitions given here show how the nonharmonic tone is approached and left in relation to the surrounding chord tones, and only secondarily, in those few cases where it is pertinent, do they show whether the dissonant tone is accented or not.

DEFINITIONS

Passing Tone

Abbreviation—*P.T.*

Figure 297

A nonharmonic tone, standing between two different chord tones, approached and left by step, in the same direction.

Neighboring Tone

Abbreviation—*N.T.*
U.N.T.
L.N.T.

Figure 298

A nonharmonic tone, standing between two occurrences of the same chord tone, approached and left by step, in different directions.

Suspension

Abbreviation—*S.*

Figure 299

A chord tone that is held across a change of harmony, becomes dissonant, and resolves by step to a chord tone.

Anticipation

Abbreviation—*Ant.*

Figure 300

A nonharmonic tone that anticipates a chord tone before a change of harmony.

Appoggiatura

Abbreviation—*App.*

Figure 301

A nonharmonic tone that is approached by skip and resolved by step to a chord tone.

Escape Tone

Abbreviation—*E.T.*

Figure 302

A nonharmonic tone that is approached by step and left by skip.

Pedal

Abbreviation—*P.*

Figure 303

A tone that is held through several chord changes, being a part of the first and last chords.

Free Tone

Abbreviation—*F.T.*

Figure 304

A nonharmonic tone that is approached and left by skip.

These brief definitions will be sufficient for the student to recognize, and employ in *analysis,* the different types of nonharmonic elaboration in a single voice line. A more detailed discussion of each type follows, with examples and some suggestions for using the various types in making harmonizations of a given melody.

PASSING TONE

The basic *passing tone* figure may be elaborated in several ways.

It may occur ascending or descending, accented or unaccented, and in any combination of one of the former two with one of the latter two.

Figure 305

However, unaccented passing tones are found more frequently than accented ones.

Double or triple passing tones may occur in two or three voices moving in parallel thirds and sixths.

Figure 306

Passing tones may occur in two or three voices in contrary as well as similar motion.

Figure 307

While most passing tones occur between chord tones a third apart, a chromatic passing tone may be used between two chord tones a major second apart.

Figure 308

A space greater than a third, between two chord tones, may be filled in with several passing tones, provided the motion is stepwise and in the same direction; it is immaterial that some of the tones passed through are chord tones.

Figure 309

The space of a fourth may be filled in with an unaccented passing tone followed by an accented passing tone.

Figure 310

Since nonharmonic tones are by definition decorative, they cannot correct deficiencies in the part writing of the essential tones. For example, the parallel octaves in (*a*) below are not corrected by the addition of the passing tone in (*b*) .

Figure 311

However, correct part writing may be made incorrect by the use of passing tones that incidentally produce parallel fifths or octaves. In the examples below (*a*) and (*c*) are correct without the passing tones; but the passing tone in (*b*) produces parallel fifths, and the passing tones in (*d*) produce parallel octaves.

Figure 312

While there are a few cases in the Bach chorales of parallelisms made between essential tones and nonharmonic tones, these occurrences are rare. When you add nonharmonic tones to your harmonizations, you must avoid both of the situations just described.

In the following examples, circle and identify the types of passing tones used; ignore those nonharmonic devices and harmonic materials which we have not yet discussed. Begin your analysis by separating the essential tones from those that are unessential. The harmonic background is identified by adding the roman numerals for the prevailing chords; the decorative passing tones (or other nonharmonic tones) will then dissonate with this background.

Figure 313. J. S. Bach, Chorale no. 196, "Da der Herr Christ zu Tische sass"

Figure 314. J. S. Bach, Chorale no. 182, "Wär'Gott nicht mit uns diese Zeit"

NEIGHBORING TONE

Neighboring tones (also called auxiliary tones) are those notes that lie adjacent to, that is, on either side of, an essential chord tone. They are sometimes called *returning* tones.

The upper neighboring tone is usually diatonic; that is, it will be a whole or half step above the essential tone, depending upon the position in the scale. It may be accented or unaccented.

Figure 315

The lower neighboring tone, either accented or unaccented, may be a diatonic half or whole step below the essential chord tone; however, it is often found as a chromatic lower neighbor, requiring an accidental.

Figure 316

While the upper or lower neighboring tone characteristically returns to the essential tone, they are often employed together with a skip from one to the other; the return to the essential tone then resolves both.

Figure 317

When employed together, as in the last example, the tones are sometimes called *changing* tones; do not confuse this term with the term *cambiata* (*see* Escape Tone, p. 186) .

Two or three neighboring tones may occur in parallel thirds and sixths.

Figure 318

They may be used in contrary, as well as similar, motion in in several parts.

Figure 319

Neighboring tones are frequently used in conjunction with passing tones.

Figure 320

While neighboring tones and passing tones are often used together in an elaborated texture, the student should be aware of the vast difference produced by these two types of nonharmonic tones in the progress of a single line. The passing tone moves the line from one point to a different one and therefore produces dynamic motion; the neighboring tone, on the other hand, is static, since it circles around the same point. The moving from one point to another goal produces the feeling of progress in the music, whereas circling around one point impedes the forward progress of the music by prolonging the same tone.

Analyze the examples below by indicating the basic harmonic background with roman numerals and circling the passing and

neighboring tones. Use the abbreviations *P.T.* and *N.T.* to
differentiate between the two. Ignore the material not yet studied.

Figure 321. J. S. Bach, Chorale no. 324, "Jesu, meine Freude"

Figure 322. J. S. Bach, Chorale no. 312, "O Gott, du frommer Gott"

SUSPENSION AND ANTICIPATION

If two lines move in similar motion and like rhythm, the effect is predominantly harmonic; the second voice slavishly follows the first at some consonant interval, usually a third or sixth.

Figure 323

The two lines can be given a certain amount of independence by having them move at different times; either line can move first. In one case, the new note in the line is delayed by prolonging the old note; in the other case, the new note is anticipated—it is immaterial whether the notes are tied or sounded again.

Figure 324

In the fifteenth century, when the parallel six-three chords of *faux bourdon* were the fashion,, the 7–6 suspension was a characteristic way of giving some independence to one of the lines.

Figure 325

By the eighteeenth century the suspension figure had become well codified; it consisted of a preparation, suspension, and resolution occurring in certain characteristic harmonies. Each type of suspension is usually identified by the numerals from figured bass, which describe the relation of the suspension and the resolution to the bass voice.

Figure 326

The preparation is consonant; the suspension is dissonant, usually occurring on an accent; the resolution is consonant. The dissonance resolves by step up or down to a chord member. The resolution downward by step is by far the most common; the upward resolving suspension is called a *retardation* by some theorists.

The 4–3 Suspension. This is the most frequently found suspension in Bach's music; it occurs characteristically in the dominant or the tonic harmonies.

Figure 327

The 9–8 Suspension. This suspension is found most often in tonic and subdominant harmonies. It is the only suspension where the note of resolution is present in another voice at the time of the suspension; it occasionally occurs in the tenor voice as 2–1, rather than the more common 9–8 in the soprano or alto voice.

Figure 328

The 7–6 Suspension. This suspension occurs in the first inversion of the tonic and leading tone triads.

Figure 329

The Suspension in the Bass. This is less frequent than the suspension in an upper part and is more difficult to identify by numerals, since the bass note (the point of reference in the figured bass) changes at the moment of resolution. It occurs in the root position ($\begin{smallmatrix}7\\4-5\\2-3\end{smallmatrix}$) and the first inversion ($\begin{smallmatrix}5-6\\2-3\end{smallmatrix}$) of the tonic and dominant triads. Both suspensions are sometimes called 2–3 suspensions, since these intervals occur with the bass and the next highest part in both.

Figure 330

Suspension with Change of Bass. Occasionally the base note will change when the suspension in an upper part resolves. This makes identification by figured bass numerals difficult, but the dissonant suspended note resolves in the usual way, one step down to a chord tone.

Figure 331

Double Suspension. It is possible to suspend two of the upper parts; both are treated as if they were single suspensions. The accented cadential six-four chord is often prepared as a double suspension.

$$I_4^9 : {8 \atop 3} \quad V_4^6 : {5 \atop 3}$$

Figure 332

Upward Resolving Suspension. While not found so frequently as the downward resolution, the upward resolving suspension is quite effective, particularly when the suspension resolves up a half step.

$$a: IV_2^5 \text{---} 3 \qquad\qquad I^7 \cdot 8$$

Figure 333

Before continuing, you should practice constructing the common suspensions (4–3, 9–8, 7–6) in different keys. First write the bass note and the figures for the suspension and its resolution. For instance, write a 4–3 suspension in the dominant harmony of the key of E flat major:

Eb: V⁴ · ³

Figure 334

Next add the suspension in one of the upper parts, then its resolution and its preparation.

Eb: V⁴ · ³

Figure 335

Complete the dominant chord, calculating the note of resolution as a chord member.

Eb: V⁴ · ³

Figure 336

Finally, harmonize the note of preparation.

Eb: I   V⁴ · ³

Figure 337

The same procedure may be applied to the other suspension types.

ANTICIPATION

While the *anticipation* is often the literal retrograde of the suspension, it is much less frequently found.

Suspension   Anticipation

Figure 338

The anticipation is probably less effective musically because it anticipates, on a weak accent, a tone from the chord on the next strong accent; in effect, it "steals" the new note before its expected appearance. Its principal use is in the melodic line at a cadence; the final tonic melody note is sometimes anticipated over the dominant harmony.

Figure 339

In the study of sixteenth-century counterpoint, the student may encounter the term *portamento*. This is the rhythmic anticipation of the note of resolution in the suspension figure; unlike the true anticipation, it is usually consonant.

Figure 340

This is a stylistic idiom of Palestrina and his contemporaries; its use is not recommended except in the study of modal counterpoint. A similar case is the *nota cambiata,* which is discussed on p. 189.

In the following chorales indicate the background harmony with roman numerals; circle and identify the passing tones (*P.T.*), neighboring tones (*N.T.*), suspensions (*S.*), and anticipations (*Ant.*). Under each suspension write the identifying numerals (4–3, 9–8, 7–6, and so on). The student should notice that the parallel fifths that occur in Chorale no. 8 occur between two unessential tones, not between an essential tone and an unessential one; in other words, if considered separately, each of the nonharmonic devices (in this case a passing tone and an anticipation) is handled correctly.

Figure 341. J. S. Bach, Chorale no. 61, "Jesu Leiden, Pein und Tod"

(continued)

Figure 342. J. S. Bach, Chorale no. 8, "Freuet euch, ihr Christen"

APPOGGIATURA AND ESCAPE TONE

The nonharmonic elaboration in the music of Bach and his contemporaries consists principally of passing tones, neighboring tones, and suspensions. The other nonharmonic devices occur sparingly; certain of them can be found in greater frequency in the music of other periods. For instance, the *appoggiatura* was more common in the period from Mozart to Brahms than in the first half of the eighteenth century, and *escape tones* were more common in medieval music than in Bach's time. For this reason we will begin to supplement the Bach examples with those from some other periods.

The appoggiatura is a dissonant tone that is *approached* by skip, while the escape tone is a dissonant tone that is *left* by skip.

Figure 343

They both maintain a stepwise connection with an essential chord tone; for this reason some texts count these as (incomplete) neighboring tones.

Characteristically, the appoggiatura is approached by skip, occurs on an accent, and is resolved by step in the opposite direction to which it was approached.

Figure 344

Figure 345. Beethoven, Sonata opus 10, no. 1

Occasionally the appoggiatura will resolve in the same direction as it is approached. This happens when a note with an upward tendency (like the leading tone) is approached from below, or a note with a downward tendency is approached from above; the line then usually changes direction and returns to the note skipped over.

Figure 346

While less frequent than the appoggiatura on the accent, the unaccented appoggiatura does occur.

Figure 347

Often the appoggiatura will be chromatically altered in the direction in which it is to resolve, that is, raised to go up or lowered to go down.

Figure 348

The escape tone is rare in eighteenth-century music, but it sometimes occurs in the cadence formula as in the following example; this is probably a truncation of a neighboring tone figure from which the final essential tone has been omitted.

Figure 349

The escape tone was a common device in some earlier periods of music; it occurs in fourteenth- and fifteenth-century music as the *Landini sixth.* This was a characteristic figure in which the sixth degree of the scale was interpolated between the seventh and the eighth scale degrees at a cadence; the sixth degree could be either consonant or dissonant with the other parts but was an unessential, or decorative, tone.

Figure 350

In the vocal music of the sixteenth century dissonance was more carefully controlled. Passing tones and neighboring tones (principally the lower neighbor) occur on unaccented beats, and the suspension is used; the appoggiatura is not found and the escape tone is limited to an idiomatic device called the *cambiata* (or *nota cambiata*).

Figure 351

The dissonant note is similar to an interrupted passing tone, the goal of which has been delayed by a consonant "lower neighbor." This is an archaic device, and its use should be limited to the study of vocal counterpoint in the style of Palestrina.

You must use some discretion in incorporating escape tones in your harmonizations. This is a rare device in recent periods of music because it defies the basic premise that dissonance is led to consonance by step. When it is found, one should examine the context carefully to see what extenuating circumstances make it effective.

Make the usual roman numeral analysis of the following chorales, and circle and identify these nonharmonic tones: P.T., N.T., S., App., and E.T.

Figure 352. J. S. Bach, Chorale no. 323, "Wie schön leuchtet der Morgenstern"

Figure 353. J. S. Bach, Chorale no. 213, "O wie selig seid ihr doch, ihr Frommen"

PEDAL, FREE TONE, COMBINATIONS

The *pedal* (sometimes called *pedal point*) is much more common in instrumental than in vocal music. There are a few examples in the Bach chorales, but it is more characteristic of nineteenth-century instrumental music.

A pedal is a sustained tone, usually in the bass, over which chord changes take place. It usually begins and ends as a consonant chord member; to be an effective pedal it should be dissonant with some of the material above it, that is, it should not always be a chord member. The voice immediately above the pedal is treated as the real bass voice, and the chords are analyzed without including the pedal note.

Figure 354

In another example, from romantic piano music, the tonic pedal in the bass is reiterated instead of being sustained.

Figure 355. Mendelssohn, "Faith," *Songs without Words,* no. 48

The pedal tone may also occur in an upper or inner part. It is excluded from the analysis except when it is a chord member.

Figure 356

In this example, also by Mendelssohn, the pedal is an inner part (the note F sharp), which is struck with each chord.

Figure 357. Mendelssohn, "Consolation," *Songs without Words,* no. 9

In instrumental music a pedal figure made up of several tones may be reiterated. This is treated in the same general way as the sustained tone.

Figure 358

The *free tone*—a dissonant note approached and left by skip—is so rare in eighteenth-century music that it is difficult to point out a clear example. Nevertheless, it is included here for the sake of completeness. You may encounter isolated cases in the analysis of medieval or twentieth-century music. It should be practically nonexistent in your own harmonizations of chorale melodies.

Figure 359

In the following example by Beethoven, the F sharp may be considered a free tone, but it probably is heard more strongly as an appoggiatura (or lower neighbor) to the note G, which, in turn, is an upper neighbor to F.

Figure 360. Beethoven, Sonata opus 22

The simultaneous use of nonharmonic tones in two or more different parts offers some interesting possibilities: one part may support another (as the passing tone in the tenor part supported the escape tone in the soprano, in the next to the last example, above), or the two parts may dissonate with each other, as well as with the prevailing harmony.

Figure 361

When a passing tone and anticipation occur together, the parallel fifths can be softened by having one of the parts move after the other.

Figure 362

The resolution note in the suspension figure is often preceded by its lower appoggiatura (or neighbor).

Figure 363

Finally, one nonharmonic tone may decorate another in a single line; in the following case an appoggiatura is attached to an upper neighboring tone.

Figure 364

Make the customary analysis of the given chorales showing the background harmony and identifying the following nonharmonic devices: P.T., N.T., S., Ant., E.T., and P.

Figure 365. J. S. Bach, Chorale no. 247, "Wenn wir in höchsten Nöten sein"

Figure 366. J. S. Bach, Chorale no. 126, "Durch Adams Fall ist ganz verderbt"

HARMONIZATIONS USING NONHARMONIC TONES

At the end of this chapter are given a number of melodies and basses to be harmonized. They should be approached in the way previously described: make an analysis of the implications inherent in the melody, sketch in the cadences and modulations, write the bass line, fill in the inner parts, and then add whatever nonharmonic decoration seems appropriate. This same general procedure is to be followed also in later chapters. The material will be cumulative, that is, to the basic vocabulary of triads the student will add nonharmonic tones, seventh chords, altered chords, and so on, in the order in which this new material is studied.

This procedure will usually be valid, at least in the beginning, for the harmonization of a chorale or a hymn type of melody where every tone is harmonized. Of course, it is not so valid a procedure for the harmonization of a more florid melody, where the decorations in the given part will affect the choice of the basic harmony. As the student gains more experience, the nonharmonic activity of the inner parts will often dictate the part writing or the position of the chord, rather than vice versa.

The following suggestions are pertinent to the decoration of a harmonization with nonharmonic tones:

1. Unless specially mentioned, it is assumed that the melody line itself, being a preexistent tune, will not be altered.

2. The most common nonharmonic devices found in eighteenth-century chorales are passing tones, neighboring tones, and suspensions; these should be used most, other devices only sparingly.

3. Too much decoration is as bad as too little. The aim of the decoration is to give some independence to the four lines rather than to produce a dense texture that is perpetually in motion. The motion usually slows down and stops at the cadence; in this chorale style the phrase customarily ends with a fermata, and there is practically no nonharmonic activity *between* phrases. As an illustration, we will add decorative material to these two phrases:

Figure 367

Passing tones usually can be placed between two chord tones a third apart. The exception to this occurs in the perfect authentic cadence where the leading tone falls to the fifth of the tonic chord; this third is not filled in with a passing tone, since this would attract attention to the fact that the leading tone did not follow its natural tendency to resolve up to the tonic.

Figure 368

Passing tones could occur between all tones a third apart in our example, with the exception of the case just mentioned, and the third that occurs between the two phrases.

Figure 369

Not all of these need be used, of course, but there is a better balance of activity if we add two suspensions to the second phrase; the possible 4–3 suspension in the final dominant chord would not be used here because it would clash with the anticipation that was given in the melody part.

Figure 370

An alternative version of the first cadence might keep some activity into the hold, but not across the two phrases. This probably should be rejected because of the parallel fifths between the alto and tenor (beats 1 to 2), and the soprano and alto (beats 2 to 3.)

Figure 371

Finally, we would examine the phrase to see where neighboring tones might be useful. Since these are static rather than forward propelling, they are chiefly useful in supporting other nonharmonic activity, like the passing tones in the anacrusic beat, or in supplying motion; in this case we might add a chromatic lower neighbor to the first beat of the last measure. The entire two phrases, decorated, would then be:

Figure 372

EXERCISES

Harmonize the following melodies and basses using triads, modulation, and nonharmonic tones.

1. "Herr, straf'mich nicht" (German chorale)

2. "Herr Jesu Christ" (German chorale)

3. "Die Nacht ist kommen" (German chorale)

4.

5.

6.

Figure 373

Chapter 14

Seventh and Ninth Chords:
Harmonic Elaboration

In the polyphonic music of the renaissance period, certain non-harmonic situations began to be used with considerable frequency; these passing tone and suspension figures tended to occur principally at cadential points. For example, a basic cadence, progressing second class, first class, tonic, was II, V, I.

Figure 374

This was then filled in with passing tones.

Figure 375

Around 1600, these dissonant nonharmonic tones began to be absorbed into the chords, becoming the first harmonic dissonances.

Figure 376

The 7-6 suspension in the first inversion of the leading-tone chord evolved into somewhat the same kind of progression, when the bass note moved at the time of the resolution.

Figure 377

The seventh-chord sonority also occurred as a suspension, or other nonharmonic decoration, within the dominant triad.

Figure 378

While Italian composers (Marenzio, Monteverdi, and Gesualdo) are sometimes credited with the first use of these sonorities, they also occur about the same time in England (Bennet and Byrd) and in Germany (Schein and Schütz). Although the seventh chord evolved from nonharmonic activity, once discovered, the seventh chord sonority then began to be used for its own sake. It was not necessarily prepared as a passing tone or suspension, but it still acknowledged its nonharmonic beginning by always resolving the dissonant chord member one step downward to a consonant tone. This necessity for resolution remains a characteristic of the seventh chord throughout most of the eighteenth and nineteenth centuries. With the breakdown of functional harmony at the end of the romantic period, and especially in the music of the impressionists, the dissonant sonorities begin to be treated as autonomous chords without the need for resolution. However, in all of the student exercises the dissonant chord member, seventh, ninth, and so on, should always resolve by step to a consonance; the specific exceptions to this will be enumerated later.

V^7 AND VII^7

The addition of the seventh to the triads on V and VII intensifies the tendency for these chords to resolve to the tonic harmony. V^7 is the most common of the seventh chords in both major and minor keys. VII^7, as a diminished seventh chord in the minor key, is frequent in Bach's music; the VII^7 in major is rather uncommon in the eighteenth century, but becomes more frequent in nineteenth-century music. Both may be used, in root position or first inversion, without the preparation of the seventh, but the seventh must resolve one step down to a chord tone; this means that the chord of resolution is most often I.

Figure 379

V^7 occurs in the cadence as a substitute for the dominant triad; it may also resolve to VI as a deceptive cadence.

Figure 380

The complete seventh chord contains four different notes; however, it commonly occurs in root position with the root doubled and the fifth omitted. The part writing into and out of the seventh chord will govern whether it is complete or not; when the V⁷ is complete, the chord before or after it may be incomplete. The incomplete chord, whether the seventh chord or one of its adjacent chords, allows the voices to move smoothly, and in some cases avoids parallel fifths.

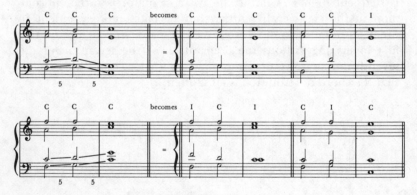

Figure 381

The dominant seventh frequently occurs in first inversion (V⁶₅), and generally is complete.

Figure 382

The second inversion, V_3^4, is somewhat less common and is subject to the same restrictions as the second inversion of the triad, that is, the dissonant fourth requires special treatment. The V_3^4 most often occurs as a passing chord between I and I^6, or vice versa. This progression must be counted as an idiom, since it is the only case in eighteenth-century style where the seventh commonly goes up.

Figure 383

The ascending form (*a*) probably grew out of the double passing tones between I and I^6. If a lower neighbor is then added to the alto part, the V_3^4 is produced by nonharmonic motion; the unequal fifths are not objectionable.

Figure 384

The third inversion (V_2^4), with the seventh in the bass, is a strong and effective position of the dominant seventh chord; it is practically always followed by I^6. Since the bass must resolve by step, the upper part sometimes makes a large skip.

Figure 385

The seventh chord on the raised leading tone in the minor key is a diminished seventh chord. Since all of the tones in the chord are separated by a minor third, all inversions sound the same acoustically, that is, like all chords built from equal intervals, it may be used freely in all inversions.

Figure 386

The chord contains two diminished fifths that have a tendency to resolve inward; this normally causes the chord to resolve to I with the third doubled.

Figure 387

However, composers have not hesitated to resolve either diminished fifth to a perfect fifth in order to get a better doubling in the tonic chord; the seventh of the chord resolves downward.

Figure 388

All inversions of the chord are usable; the third inversion normally goes to I_4^6 which, in turn, must then resolve.

Figure 389

The diminished seventh chord on the leading tone also may be used in the major key; this, of course, requires lowering the seventh of the chord with an accidental. The resolution of the chord, in all inversions, is exactly like the examples just given for the minor key.

Figure 390

The leading-tone seventh chord in the major key is a half-diminished seventh chord. In the eighteenth century it is rare; it occurs in the Bach chorales principally as a passing chord. Following the tradition of the diminished triad, the VII⁷ is often used in the first inversion (VII⁶₅); however, with its greater use in the nineteenth century, it is also found in root position. The seventh is resolved down, and the resolution chord is practically always the tonic; in fact, it might be said that it is a neighbor-note chord to I. The chord is more effective when the seventh is in the upper part.

Figure 391

Notice, in the resolution chord, that the third may be doubled. When it is not, care must be taken to avoid parallel fifths; the diminished fifth may resolve to a perfect fifth, or one of the parts must skip.

Occasionally this sonority will be produced by an appoggiatura, which resolves while the other chord tones remain, as in the following example:

Figure 392

This is more properly analyzed as a nonharmonic decoration of the dominant seventh chord.

In analyzing the examples from literature, the student will have the problem of deciding whether a particular case is best called a seventh chord or simply a triad with nonharmonic decoration. Theorists often arrive at seemingly conflicting statistics because they do not agree upon this distinction. Each case must be decided in context, and often such things as harmonic rhythm have a great deal to do with the chord feeling. For illustration, the following examples are best analyzed as seventh chords:

Figure 393

while the following somewhat similar cases are usually called triads with passing tones:

Figure 394

The distinction seems to be that in the first case the seventh lasts for the entire duration of the chord, whereas in the second the seventh enters as a nonharmonic tone after the triadic feeling has been established. Some other cases are not so easy to decide.

Figure 395

In (*a*) above, the choice is between analyzing V as a triad followed by an appoggiatura or, probably better, as a triad followed by a seventh chord on the second half of the beat; in (*b*) the eighth notes, which could be called a passing and a neighboring tone, make a VII⁷ chord on the last half of the beat. In this latter case, if the nonharmonic tones make a clearly functional chord, we will choose that analysis over the one of diverse nonharmonic tones.

Find the first-class seventh chords in the following examples, and designate each with the correct roman numerals and arabic figures (V⁷, V$^6_5$, VII⁷, VII$^6_5$, and so on). These may occur in the tonic key, or in a modulation to some related key.

Figure 396. J. S. Bach, Chorale no. 65, "Was Gott tut, das ist wohlgetan"

Figure 397. J. S. Bach, Chorale no. 92, "O Jesu Christ, du höchstes Gut"

II⁷ AND IV⁷

The second-class seventh chords on II and IV resolve to first-class chords; most often they resolve to V or V⁷. The following are common cadence formulas in the eighteenth century:

Figure 398

In the major key the supertonic seventh chord in root position resolves to V or V⁷, as in this example:

Figure 399

The chord has much less use in root position in the minor key because of the diminished fifth with the bass; however, Bach occasionally uses the root position after the first inversion. The skip in the bass is apparently used to supply motion on the second half of the beat.

Figure 400

The first inversion of the supertonic seventh chord, in both major and minor keys, is the most common position of this chord. This makes possible a strong bass line moving subdominant, dominant, tonic, in the progression II$^6_5$ V I; this is the most frequently found cadential approach in eighteenth-century style.

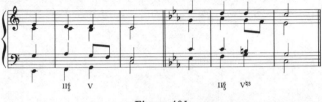

Figure 401

The second inversion of the supertonic seventh chord is of negligible importance. The third inversion occurs with the

seventh of the chord resolving down to the leading tone in the
bass; this is a strong approach to V or V⁷ in first inversion.

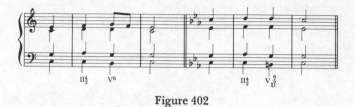

Figure 402

IV⁷ in root position is sometimes used as the approach to V in
the authentic cadence, in both major and minor keys; the part
writing of this progression requires special attention. When a
seventh chord resolves to a triad a second above it, the third is
usually doubled in the resolution chord; this avoids both sets of
parallel fifths that might occur with other part writing.

Figure 403

However, this part writing is not possible in the progression
IV⁷ V, since the third of V is the leading tone, and this sensitive
tone is rarely doubled. Bach uses one of the following procedures:
IV⁷ goes to V with a doubled fifth (this requires a large skip in
one part) or he progresses through a passing tone to V⁷. Either
procedure may occur in either the major or minor key.

Figure 404

The first inversion of the subdominant seventh chord occurs when the bass voice has an ascending line up to the tonic. It is preceded by III or I and is followed by V; in the minor key, the ascending form of the melodic minor scale is used.

Figure 405

As with most seventh chords, the second inversion is rarely found. The third inversion occurs when the ascending scale line up to the tonic is in an upper part. The chord is preceded by III or I and is followed by the leading tone triad in first inversion (VII⁶); again, the ascending melodic form of the minor scale is used.

Figure 406

In the following examples, identify the first- and second-class seventh chords; these may occur in the principal key or in a related key.

(continued)

Figure 407. J. S. Bach, Chorale no. 190, "Herr, nun lass in Frieden"

Figure 408. J. S. Bach, Chorale no. 239, "Den Vater dort oben"

VI⁷, I⁷, AND III⁷

The remaining possible seventh chords on VI, I, and III are rarely found in eighteenth-century music; indeed they are rare in any period, since they are far removed from the tonic triad in the circle of fifths. The addition of the seventh to these triads, however, can act as an intensifier to make the chords move to the next classification.

Figure 409

Of course, such laboratory progressions occur rarely in music, at least in such a complete form, but segments of the circle of fifths can be found.

You should now review the chart of strong progressions given on p. 149. The root movements down a fifth or up a second give the note of resolution for the seventh added to a triad.

Figure 410

This means that VI⁷ is normally followed by II, or sometimes VII in the first inversion, I⁷ is followed by IV or II, and III⁷ will go to VI or IV.

Figure 411

In the following examples from the Bach chorales, find and
label all of the seventh chords. Distinguish between a triad decorated with a nonharmonic tone and a seventh chord that resolves on a change of root.

Figure 412. J. S. Bach, Chorale no. 39, "Ach was soll ich Sünder machen"

Figure 413. J. S. Bach, Chorale no. 26, "O Ewigkeit, du Donnerwort"

Figure 414. J. S. Bach, Chorale no. 12, "Puer natus in Bethlehem"

Figure 415. J. S. Bach, Chorale no. 145, "Warum betrübst du dich"

NINTH CHORDS

Alfredo Cassella, writing in the early years of this century, remarks that the dominant major ninth chord "is, without any doubt, the greatest harmonic discovery of the nineteenth century."[1] While the sonority is certainly characteristic of much nineteenth-century composition, particularly the later works, it still plays a less important role than many harmony books have suggested, and the harmonic vocabulary of the nineteenth century still consists primarily of triads and seventh chords.

The major and minor dominant ninth chords are created by the addition of a third to the usual dominant seventh chords; the resolution is generally to I.

Figure 416

The first examples of the minor ninth, although rare, can be found in instrumental music as far back as Bach.

[1] Alfredo Cassella, *The Evolution of Music through the History of the Perfect Cadence* (London: J. & W. Chester, 1924), p. 17.

Figure 417. J. S. Bach, Prelude no. 12, *Well-tempered Clavier*

Since the upper part of the ninth chord in the minor key formed the diminished seventh chord (♮VII⁷), composers often used this as if it were a separate chord above a dominant pedal.

Figure 418. Beethoven, Sonata opus 10, no. 1

Since the complete ninth chord requires five notes, this chord could be more easily accommodated in the multivoice texture of instrumental music than in four-part vocal writing. It begins to appear sparingly in the instrumental writing of Beethoven and Schubert in both major and minor keys, but subject at first to some restrictions.

The sonority goes through several stages of development growing out of nonharmonic activity above the dominant seventh chord before its final acceptance as an independent chord. The development took place first in the minor key, and later in the major key; the following kinds of resolution of the ninth can be found in the instrumental music of the early nineteenth century:

1. The ninth occurs as an appoggiatura to the root of the dominant seventh chord.

Figure 419

In five parts this becomes:

Figure 420

At this stage the ninth is a nonharmonic decoration of V⁷, and is resolved to the dominant chord before the dominant chord resolves to the tonic.

2. The appoggiatura ninth goes on to the seventh, which then resolves.

Figure 421

Or in five parts:

Figure 422

This figure is then abbreviated:

Figure 423

At this stage it appears as if the ninth receives no resolution; however, the ninth to seventh results from a truncation of the activity within the seventh chord. It is clear that what is being resolved in this case is the dominant seventh chord.

3. The third stage accepts the ninth as a harmonic member of the dominant chord. The ninth then regularly resolves to a consonance in the next chord in the same manner as the seventh.

Figure 424

4. The last stage (reached before the middle of the nineteenth century) finds the dominant ninth chord in instrumental music treated as an autonomous chord where the ninth receives no direct resolution, but the chord is considered resolved when it is followed by a tonic chord.

Figure 425

These four types of resolution may be illustrated from nineteenth-century instrumental literature. First, the ninth as appoggiatura to V⁷ can be seen in the *Unfinished* Symphony of Schubert.

Figure 426. Schubert, Symphony no. 8 (*Unfinished*)

Then the second stage, when the ninth moves to the seventh and then resolves.

Figure 427. Schubert, Sonata opus 122

In the third stage the ninth of the chord resolves in the same voice to another chord.

Figure 428. Mendelssohn, "Faith," *Songs without Words*, no. 48

Finally, the dominant ninth chord is considered to be resolved when it is followed by the tonic chord; the ninth of the chord may be resolved in some other part.

Figure 429. Chopin, Prelude opus 28, no. 7

Figure 430. Beethoven, Piano Concerto no. 3

Probably only the last two stages should be considered as real
ninth chords, since the first two stages result from nonharmonic
activity within the seventh chord, but theorists have frequently
called all of these stages ninth chords without distinguishing
between them. Once the sonority of the ninth chord was recognized, all of the types of resolution were freely used throughout
most of the nineteenth century.

In four-part texture the fifth of the chord, as the least necessary tone, is usually omitted. The root position and first inversion
are the most frequently found; the third inversion is rare. The
minor ninth may resolve to either the major or minor tonic; the
major ninth resolves only to the major tonic chord.

Figure 431

In four-part writing the ninth should resolve in the same voice
to a consonant chord member.

ELEVENTH AND THIRTEENTH CHORDS

In the latter half of the nineteenth century, composers continued the process of superimposing thirds over the dominant
chord. The eleventh and thirteenth chords, so named from the
intervals of the last added tone above the roots, occur only
rarely, but supply certain characteristic sonorities of instrumental
music in this romantic period.

Figure 432

Brünhilde's motive from *Götterdämmerung*, the last opera of *The Ring* by Wagner, outlines the dominant eleventh chord.

Figure 433. Wagner, *Götterdämmerung*

The eleventh chord is found less frequently than the other dominant discords, probably because the eleventh is the tonic note sounding over the dominant chord. The eleventh may resolve to the leading tone while the dominant chord remains, making it in reality an appoggiatura to V^9, or else it is held in the same voice into the chord of resolution.

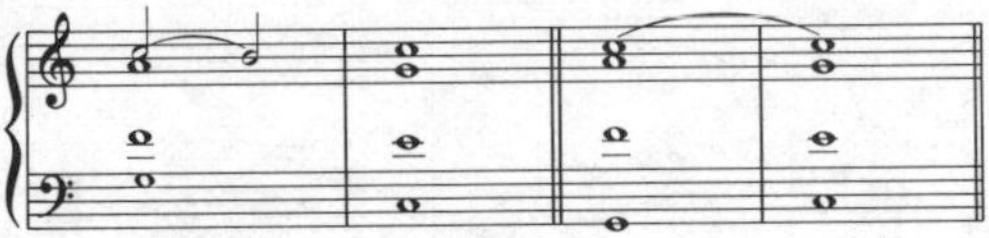

Figure 434

This latter case sounds like a subdominant chord in the upper parts over a dominant bass note; this is somewhat like a combination plagal-authentic cadence. An interesting example from literature can be found at the important cadence on the dominant in *Prélude à l'Après-midi d'un faune;* the V^{11} is decorated with nonharmonic tones.

Figure 435. Debussy, *Prélude à l'Après-midi d'un faune*

The dominant thirteenth chord is actually more common than the eleventh chord, since the chord is probably derived from the appoggiatura to the fifth of the dominant seventh chord.

Figure 436

When the thirteenth resolves to the fifth of V⁷, it is more properly called an appoggiatura than a chord member, even though the resolution is delayed until the last moment, as in this example from Chopin.

Figure 437. Chopin, Prelude opus 28, no. 3

The true thirteenth receives no stepwise resolution but skips directly to the tonic note, or remains to be the third in the tonic chord. This becomes a common approach to the cadence in late nineteenth-century music.

Figure 438. Schumann, "Traümerei"

Figure 439. Brahms, "Immer leiser wird mein Schlummer"

Figure 440. Franck, Symphony in D minor

In the following excerpt from the Franck Violin Sonata, label all of the examples of the higher dominant discords (ninth, eleventh, and thirteenth).

Figure 441. Franck, Violin Sonata

EXERCISES

A. Harmonize, in four parts, the following chorale melodies, using triads and seventh chords in root position and appropriate inversions. Nonharmonic tones may also be used, but special attention should be given to the use of seventh chords and their proper resolution.

1. "Jesu Leiden, Pein und Tod" (German chorale)

2. "Durch Adams Fall" (German chorale)

3. "Nun ruhen alle Wälder" (German chorale)

4. "Auf, auf, mein Herz" (German chorale)

5. "Ihr Gestirn', ihr hohlen Lüfte" (German chorale)

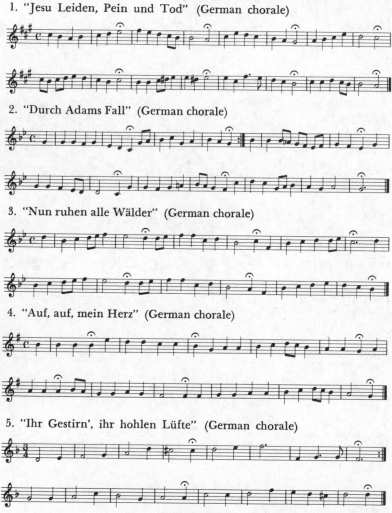

Figure 442

B. After reading Chapter 16, add the upper three voices to the given
figured basses; pay particular attention to the resolution of dissonant
chord members.

Figure 443

Chapter 15

Altered Chords and
Chromaticism (Tonal Elaboration)

One of the objections to the conventional theory of harmony
that Hindemith raises is that "by raising or lowering tones of the
diatonic scales the chord-supply of a key may be enriched."[1]
Hindemith implies that, historically, the principle of alteration,
when it applied to only a few tones of a scale, was a valid one,
but that, when the alterations became very numerous, the theory
of the diatonic scale with alterations should have been given up
in favor of the multitone scale.

The problem that Hindemith points out is twofold: partly,
it stems from our antiquated system of notation, which attempts
to represent twelve sounds with seven letter names, and, in addition, there is a psychological problem in perception—of perceiv-
ing a "diatonic" scale in multitone music. Although the twelve-
tone scale was in actual use by the time of *Tristan und Isolde,*
about 1860, the earlier theory of a diatonic seven-tone scale with
alterations still persisted. The student needs to understand this
earlier theory, not only for historical reasons, but because it is
still an adequate and plausible way of describing music that is
predominately diatonic. The following discussion of altered
chords is based upon conventional explanations of the altered
tones occurring in tonal music that uses the major-minor key
signatures. (The student should review Chapter 7.) Concepts
applicable to more recent tonal music that uses the multitone
scale are discussed below under The Twelve-Tone Scale.

---

[1] Paul Hindemith, *The Craft of Musical Composition,* rev. ed. (New York:
Associated Music Publishers, 1945) , p. 90.

THE PRINCIPLE OF MELODIC ALTERATION

The earliest examples of altered tones in a melodic line go back to medieval music, when the terms *musica ficta* or *musica falsa* were used to describe occasional tones that were outside the prevailing seven-tone modal scale. These "fictitious" or "false" notes were considered to be degrees of the diatonic mode altered by an accidental. The alterations were basically of two types: the B flat used as a close upper neighbor note to the tone A, and the raised leading tone in the final cadence of the Dorian, Mixolydian, and Aeolian modes.[2]

Both alterations illustrate the same principle: the tendency of a tone to resolve, either up or down, is intensified by altering the tone a half step in the direction toward which it is to resolve. Obviously this applies primarily to two tones a whole step apart.

Figure 444

Figure 445

[2] Of the remaining modes (disregarding the Locrian), the Lydian and Ionian modes already contain a half step between the seventh and eighth degrees; the Phrygian mode exhibits the inversion of this cadence, placing the half step between the second and first degrees, and the whole step between the seventh and eighth.

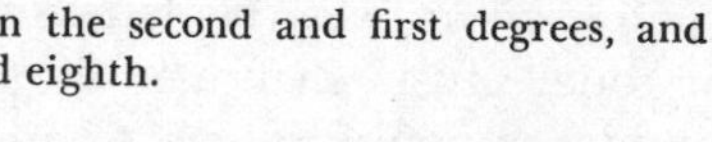

Figure 446

The B flat was used also for another purpose, that is, to soften an actual or implied tritone in a melodic line that contained the tones B and F.

This practice of alteration is most commonly found today in the minor scale, where the seventh degree is customarily raised, when it ascends to the tonic. A related situation occurs in the melodic form of the minor scale, when a tone is altered to remove the augmented second of the harmonic minor scale.

Figure 447

The basic principle of alteration, for melodic purposes, is that one alters a tone in the direction in which it is to go. This alteration functions like a leading tone (or an inverted leading tone, as in the Phrygian mode) pulling toward the following tone. Stated another way, the melodic pull of the minor second is stronger than that of the major second, in moving a melodic line toward a goal. When these altered melodic tones become part of a chord, they produce altered chords. Practically all altered chords are derived from the melodic bending of a chord member; the very few exceptions to this, where alterations are made primarily for harmonic reasons, will be discussed later under Harmonic Alterations (p. 243).

RAISED TONES: SECONDARY DOMINANTS, AUGMENTED TRIADS

The quasi-leading tone may be supported by a dominant sounding chord; this sonority is often called a *secondary dominant* to the chord of resolution. This theory implies that no real modulation has been effected, but that the drive toward the diatonic chord is intensified by the altered tone. Any of the major or minor triads in either the major or minor key may be preceded by its own first-class sonority; the term *secondary dominant* in most theory books is meant to include the sonority types of V, V⁷, VII, VII⁷, and so on.

Figure 448

In the following example the diatonic triads labeled with roman numerals are preceded by secondary dominants. The increased pull of the altered tones may be tested out by first playing through the exercise and omitting all of the accidentals.

Figure 449

The augmented triad, which also exhibits the altered-tone principle, probably grew out of a chromatic passing tone.

Figure 450

In time the augmented triad was accepted as an independent sonority; it no longer showed its passing tone origin, but the altered tone continued to resolve up.

Figure 451

This chord occurs most commonly in the major key on I, IV, or V; the altered tone is not doubled.

Figure 452

In the minor key the augmented triad frequently is found on III, supporting the raised leading tone.

Figure 453

When the augmented chord on III in minor occurs in first inversion, it is a first-class chord, that is, it functions like V ♮3, the sixth above the bass being a substitute for the fifth.

Figure 454

In the following phrase from a Bach chorale both a secondary
dominant (V ♮ ³ of IV), and an augmented triad (VI ♮ ⁵) occur
in the tonic key of G minor.

Figure 455. J. S. Bach, Chorale no. 203, "O Mensch"

LOWERED TONES: LOWERED SIXTH DEGREE, NEAPOLITAN CHORD

The opposite case occurs when a scale degree is lowered in
order to intensify the melodic motion downward. The sixth
degree of the major scale is sometimes depressed to increase its
tendency to resolve to the fifth degree. This is sometimes described in theory books as "borrowing" the IV, or II, chord from
the tonic (or parallel) minor key.

Figure 456

A clear case of borrowing occurs in the deceptive cadence
where a major submediant chord, built on lowered VI, is used
in the major key.

Figure 457

The complete submediant chord, in this case, is borrowed from the tonic minor key; the fermata of the cadence obscures any melodic reason for the alterations.

In the minor key, the lowered second degree, as a part of the *Neapolitan 6 chord,* has been a common alteration since the seventeenth century.

Figure 458

The melodic origin of this alteration is shown by the soprano line in the above example; the principal tone C is surrounded by its upper and lower neighbor notes, each of which has been altered to make it closer to the principal tone. This derivation is still apparent when the lowered supertonic skips to the raised leading tone; the tonic note then resolves both. The cross relation between the soprano D ♭ and the tenor D ♮ is commonly found.

Figure 459

Sometimes, perhaps to soften the cross-relation effect, a passing diminished seventh chord is placed between the Neapolitan 6 chord and the dominant.

Figure 460

Later in the baroque period, the Neapolitan 6 chord was carried over into the major key as a harmonic unit. This, of course,
required the lowered sixth as well as the lowered second degree;
the chord was still usually found in first inversion. As in all examples of the Neapolitan 6 chord, the third of the chord is
doubled.

Figure 461

In the nineteenth century the Neapolitan chord is also used in
root position, as well as the more conventional first inversion.

Figure 462. Chopin, Prelude opus 28, no. 20

Examples of these altered chords from the baroque periods are
more restrained, but the following phrases from two Bach chorales show the lowered sixth scale degree.

1. J. S. Bach, Chorale no. 6, "Christus, der ist mein Leben"

2. J. S. Bach, Chorale no. 139, "Warum sollt' ich"

Figure 463

The only example of the Neapolitan 6 chord in the Bach chorales is resolved through a diminished seventh chord, before going to the dominant.

Figure 464. J. S. Bach, Chorale no. 262, "Ach Gott, vom Himmel"

RAISED AND LOWERED TONES: AUGMENTED SIXTH CHORDS, THE ALTERED DOMINANT CHORD, OTHER FUNCTIONS

In the baroque period, the so-called *augmented sixth chords* probably originated in the minor key as second-class chords utilizing a raised fourth scale degree that subsequently resolved up to the fifth. Harmony books have traditionally used the descriptive names Italian, French, and German to differentiate three sonority types; each of them contained the interval of the augmented sixth between the sixth and the raised fourth scale degrees, in the minor key.

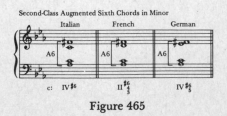

Figure 465

These sonorities, originally produced by melodic voice leading, were then treated as autonomous chords in both minor and major keys. When they occur in the major key, they require both the raising of the fourth degree and the lowering of the sixth degree to produce the augmented sixth; the German type also requires lowering the third degree.

Figure 466

The melodic origin of these chords stems from the secondary leading tone to V, in the minor key.

Figure 467

In the cadence formula, the second-class chord could be either the subdominant or the supertonic chord; the different dispositions of the inner parts produced the three different types of augmented sixth chord.

The Italian augmented sixth chord is the simplest sonority, containing only three pitches; the inner note is doubled. The raised four is often preceded by a suspension; the resolution is to V ♮ ³.

Figure 468

The French type is made from the supertonic seventh chord; its characteristic sound contains two tritones. The resolution is also to V ♮ ³

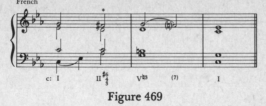

Figure 469

The German type, derived from the subdominant seventh chord, usually goes through a I_4^6 chord before resolving to V ♮ ³ in order to avoid the pair of consecutive perfect fifths that would otherwise occur between the alto and bass voices.

Figure 470

Another way of avoiding these parallel fifths is to resolve the upper tone of the fifth first; this, in effect, produces a French augmented sixth before the chord of resolution.

Figure 471

The second-class augmented sixth chords in the major key are exactly similar; the last four examples may be played in the major key with the necessary changes in accidentals.

The German type in major may be found written two ways, either as a subdominant seventh chord, or as a supertonic seventh chord.

Figure 472

The last spelling is more logical if the resolution is through the I$_4^6$ chord to V.

Figure 473

Nineteenth-century composers continued to utilize these second-class augmented sixth chords and also, treating the chords as autonomous sonorities, used the same sounds as first-class chords. The first-class augmented sixth chords are derived from V or VII and resolve to I; they occur in both major and minor keys.

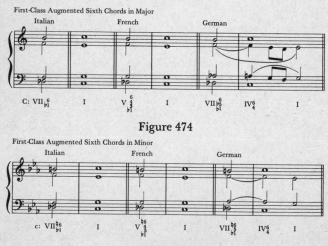

Figure 474

Figure 475

The transferring of the augmented sixth sonorities to the first-class function focused attention upon the possibilities of other alterations to V or V⁷. The most practical alterations were the raised and lowered fifth, since any other alterations tended to change the function of the chord. These two alterations made a variety of first-class sonorities available to the nineteenth-century composer. The following possibilities are frequently found; they all customarily resolve to I, or to some other substitute that can accommodate the resolution of the altered tones.

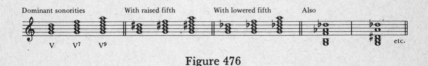

Figure 476

The upper part of these dominant sonorities also functioned as chords built on the leading tone (VII).

Figure 477

All these altered V or VII chords contained one or more tritones in their makeup; these tritone sonorities became a strongly characteristic sound of late nineteenth-century music. Once discovered, these tritone sounds were then constructed on the other functions of a key, somewhat like altered secondary dominants.

Earlier, in predominantly diatonic music, the harmonies of different functions had different characteristic sounds in both the major and minor keys. For example, consider the sonorities in the following chord progression in both major and minor keys:

Figure 478

Figure 479

When the tritone sonorities are applied to these other functions, all of the chords begin to sound like "secondary dominants," with or without alterations. The same two progressions
might have been written in the nineteenth century with these
alterations:

Figure 480

When this stage of evolution was reached, it was no longer
possible to equate sonority with function. One could no longer
speak of a tonic seventh chord, a supertonic seventh chord, or a
dominant seventh chord on the basis of sonority alone, since all
of these functions might have the same "secondary dominant"
sound. The real difference between chords became one of *tension*

and *direction;* the composer maintained a degree of tension throughout a progression by means of seventh chords and altered chords, and relaxed this tension with a triad at cadences or structural points.

HARMONIC ALTERATION

The melodic alterations just described first appeared in the renaissance and early baroque periods when the emphasis was upon the contrapuntal dimension of music; the rationale of these alterations is to be found in the melodic conduct of the single line. Later, in the baroque, classic, and romantic periods, when the emphasis was more harmonic than contrapuntal, the vertical sonorities that the melodic alterations had produced were then used for their own sake.

The simplest illustration of this is the case of the raised leading tone in minor that produces a major dominant triad. This raised leading tone in the contrapuntal period always resolved up to the tonic; by Bach's time, when it appears in an inner voice, it frequently falls to the fifth of the tonic chord. For example:

Figure 481

In the contrapuntal period the voice leading of (*a*) is preferred; in the Bach chorales both procedures are found, but (*b*) is slightly more common. Bach prefers the complete tonic chord to the incomplete tonic that results from voice leading (*a*); or, to put it another way, in (*b*) the major dominant chord is being used per se, regardless of the part writing into and out of it.

Similar occurrences can be found for secondary dominant and secondary leading-tone chords. In one of the Bach examples quoted above, a diminished seventh chord was inserted between the Neapolitan 6 chord and the dominant.

Figure 482

The E natural in the tenor voice seems to be raised to go up, but then resolves down. It is clear in this case that Bach is primarily interested in the vertical sonority of the leading-tone seventh chord of V.

A related occurrence is:

Figure 483. J. S. Bach, Chorale no. 59, "Herzliebster Jesu"

Again, the voice leading in the individual parts is subordinated to the desired vertical sonority: in this case, the secondary dominant of V.

In the following phrase from Bach's setting of the chorale "Es ist genug," the parallel sevenths between the third and fourth chords appear to be somewhat unusual.

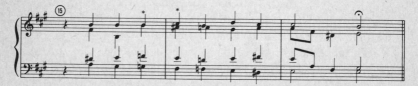

Figure 484. J. S. Bach, Chorale no. 216, "Es ist genug"

If the tenor part is respelled as a part of the Italian augmented sixth chord, and allowed to ascend, then the original contrapuntal voice leading is not so unorthodox. Compare the following contrapuntal version with that of Bach:

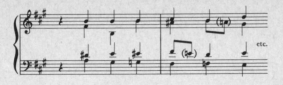

Figure 485

Bach's version is much more succinct, and emphasizes the vertical harmonic structures that occur over the descending chromatic scale line in the bass part.

If one looks at nineteenth-century music it becomes increasingly clear that the composers are more concerned with the altered chord sonorities than with the voice leading that produced them. Sometimes the desired sonorities are principally triads, as in this example from *The Ring:*

Figure 486. Wagner, *Die Walküre*

At other times the dissonant tritone sonorities with a dominant, or secondary dominant, function seem to dominate the music.

Figure 487. Wagner, *Die Walküre*

It is at this point that Hindemith's observation becomes pertinent; the chord supply of the "diatonic" key had become so
"enriched" with alterations that the original chord functions became obscure. Any one of the sonority types in this nineteenth-
century harmonic vocabulary—triads, seventh chords, ninth
chords, and altered chords—could then be constructed on any
root. At first these roots were diatonic scale degrees, but other
types of root movement appeared; especially characteristic were
roots a major or minor second, a major or minor third, or a
tritone apart.

Figure 488. Dvorak, Symphony no. 5

Figure 489. Mussorgsky, *Boris Godunov*

How this type of root movement was organized around the tonic will be discussed below, under The Twelve-Tone Scale.

Finally, the nineteenth-century composer discovered that new harmonic sounds could be produced by writing appoggiaturas to existing chords. The best known example of this is probably the beginning of the Prelude to Wagner's *Tristan und Isolde*.

Figure 490. Wagner, *Tristan und Isolde*

The characteristic sonorities of this famous passage depend upon stressing, either by length or accent, the two appoggiaturas to the supertonic and dominant chords in the key of A minor. While it would be difficult to exhaust all of the possible sonorities that could be made from this principle, the following are typical. They are produced by making appoggiaturas a half step or a whole step, above or below, members of familiar triads and seventh chords.

Figure 491

While many examples of such appoggiatura chords occur in compositions of the romantic period, the following song by Grieg contains characteristic and typical sonorities of this type. Analyze the basic chord structures and indicate the appoggiaturas, suspensions, and passing tones.

Figure 492. Grieg, "Ich liebe dich"

REMOTE MODULATION

Modulation was defined earlier as the process by which one changed keys in a composition. The process is most effective when the "keys" are seven-tone major or minor scales, or other tonal areas consisting of relatively few tones. In eighteenth-century practice the process usually extended only to what were termed *closely related keys,* that is, modulations were usually confined to those keys with one more, or one less, accidental in the key signature.

Exceptionally in the eighteenth century, and more commonly in the nineteenth, composers then extended the process to include more remote keys, as the tonal elaboration became more complex. While it is possible, in late nineteenth-century music, to find examples of modulations from a given key to practically any other key, it is convenient to systematize the remote modulations around one of the following three principles, or some combination of them.

By Change of Mode (Major-Minor). With the raised leading tone firmly established as the norm in the baroque period, the major dominant triad functioned as a common chord between a major key and its tonic minor key, or vice versa.

(continued)

Figure 493

The dominant triad, or seventh chord, was the means of exit and entry from one key to another that was three accidentals removed in key signature. The following portion of a duet from Act II of *The Marriage of Figaro* shows a clear example of an eighteenth-century use of this principle:

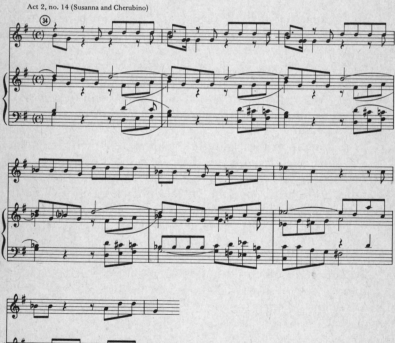

Figure 494. Mozart, *The Marriage of Figaro*

When combined with the following principle, the principle of modulation by change of mode also gave access to all of the closely related keys of the parallel key signature.

Chain Modulation. Chain modulation arrives at a distant key by two, or more, closely related key changes, that is, after progressing through several closely related keys a composition may arrive at a more distantly related key. In the process one of the steps may be a modulation by change of mode.

In the examples following, (1), starting in C major, arrives at the key of D major (two accidentals removed) by going through G major (a closely related key); (2), also starting in C major, arrives at the key of E flat major by going through C minor (a change of mode).

1.

2.

Figure 495

The Chromatic Third-Relation. The music of the nineteenth century shows many examples of chord progressions in which the root moves a major or minor third up or down. Characteristically, the sonority type (major triad, minor triad, major-minor seventh chord, and so on) is the same for both chords.

Figure 496

This type of progression is frequently called *chromatic third-relation,* to distinguish it from the third-related diatonic progressions that occur within a major or minor key. The chromatic third-relation occurs in seventeenth- and eighteenth-century music, and with increasing frequency in the nineteenth century. The composer of the romantic period then uses this chord progression as a means of entering a distant key.

The progressions can be systematized as follows, using major triads as the examples:

1. The root moves up, or down, a major, or minor, third.
2. The common tone is kept.
3. One part moves a chromatic half step.
4. The remaining part moves diatonically.

Figure 497

The same procedures may be applied to minor triads, seventh chords, and so on.

When this progression is used as the entry into a new key, it is sometimes called *modulation through a common tone.* The common tone is all that remains of the "process" of changing key; once the new chord is reached it is treated in the new key.

In the well-known song, "Widmung" (Devotion), by Schumann, this process is used to leave the key of A flat major and to enter E major, a chromatic third-relation. The tonic note in bar 13 is retained in the following measure as a common tone, which is enharmonically respelled (A flat = G sharp). In the return to the principal key, A flat major, in bar 26, C sharp is treated as the enharmonic common tone, D flat.

(continued)

Figure 498. Schumann, "Widmung"

Finally, you should analyze the Schumann song "Die Lotos-blume" and the piano reduction of the excerpt from Symphony no. 1 by Johannes Brahms, which are given below. They contain examples of altered chords and chromatic modulations that are typical of the romantic vocabulary.

(*continued*)

Figure 499. Schumann, "Die Lotosblume"

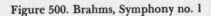

Figure 500. Brahms, Symphony no. 1

The twelve-tone scale

In the latter half of the nineteenth century, composers became increasingly interested in the possibilities and challenges afforded by the multitone scale. Josef Rufer gives an interesting account of a study that he made of the thematic material used in selected nineteenth- and early twentieth-century works.[1] He found that many of the themes of this period contained ten, eleven, or twelve different pitches, rather than the seven or eight tones characteristic of earlier periods. These multitone works were tonal, that is, although they utilized tones outside the seven-tone key signature, they were oriented toward one principal tonic.

The earliest attempts to analyze this multitone music by compromise theories based on the major-minor scale have been reviewed above (modulation, secondary dominants, altered chords, and so on). We must now find more realistic ways of categorizing this more complicated tonality. Heinrich Schenker, in his book *Harmony,* published anonymously in 1906, suggested that the amalgamation of the major and minor scales on the same tonic was already a fact, and advocated showing this by the designation, $C \frac{\text{major}}{\text{minor}}$.[2] This was a ten-tone scale.

Figure 501

Schenker believed that the major or minor triads on I, IV, and V of a key existed as coloristic variants of these functions. These ten tones also made possible numerous other triads and seventh chords outside the seven-tone scale.

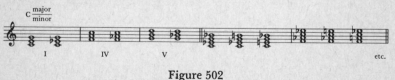

Figure 502

[1] Josef Rufer, *Composition With Twelve Notes,* trans. Humphrey Searle (London: Barrie and Rockliff, 1961) , chap. 2, pp. 14–23.

[2] Heinrich Schenker, *Harmony,* trans. Elizabeth Mann Borgese, ed. Oswald Jonas (Chicago: The University of Chicago Press, 1954) , p. 86.

The two missing pitches of the possible twelve, D flat and F sharp in the scale of C, frequently occurred in the Neapolitan 6 chord, or in the secondary dominant to V. Thus, all of the twelve pitches were being used by the latter half of the nineteenth century, but it became increasingly apparent that the theories concerning their use were inadequate and in need of revision.

Possibly a more realistic way of thinking about the organization of the twelve pitches in tonal music was suggested by Paul Hindemith in 1937, in Book I of *The Craft of Musical Composition*.[3] Hindemith believed that any theory of tonal music should start with the twelve possible pitches of the tempered scale, rather than with seven, or some smaller number. These twelve pitches, freely written in enharmonic notation, were then organized around one tonal center. The tonal center was emphasized by several factors—duration, accent, the first and last notes, the tone most often returned to, and so on—but principally by the relative strength of the root movement surrounding it. The relative harmonic strength of the root movement was measured by a chart of intervals that Hindemith called Series 2. This listed the simple harmonic intervals, excluding the octave and the tritone, in a descending order of harmonic strength: perfect fifth, perfect fourth, major third, minor sixth, minor third, major sixth, major second, and minor second.

Figure 503

Hindemith suggests that a musical composition can be analyzed by grouping the tones into chords or harmonic cells, separating the nonharmonic elements, and then extracting the roots of these chords. The chord roots are placed on a staff and from these the tonic is found.

While Hindemith's ideas have been criticized, especially the logic of the mathematics and acoustics in the early chapters of the book, his theories of practical analysis have much to recommend them. Eventually, you should read through *The Craft of*

3 Paul Hindemith, *The Craft of Musical Composition.*

Musical Composition, study the analyses given, and then attempt to make similar analyses, particularly of romantic or contemporary tonal compositions that use a multitone scale. Certainly one of the real advantages that Hindemith advocates is the realistic recognition of twelve real tones in the tempered scale, as opposed to earlier theories of "altered" diatonic functions.

Other important theories concerning the organization of romantic music were proposed by Heinrich Schenker, particularly in his last work, *Der freie Satz,* published in 1935. Schenker believed that every tonal work in the last analysis was an unfolding of the elaborated tonic chord. The basic melodic line (the *Urlinie*) moved resolutely, by step, from some member of the tonic chord to the final tonic note, while the harmonic setting (the *Ursatz*) always involved the fundamental progression I V I.

Figure 504

This basic harmonic structure, which was really an arpeggiation of the tonic chord, was sometimes elaborated by the use of II, III, IV, or VI placed before the V chord, and supporting an elaborated melodic line.

Figure 505

Schenker also advocated making the analysis of a composition on different levels; he used the terms *foreground, middle ground,* and *background.* The forground consisted of the level of detailed elaboration—the notes of the actual composition. Much of this detail was then suppressed, in order to move to the middle ground, and to show the meaning behind the elaboration. The background, after further elimination of detail, showed the basic harmonic structure of the work. This idea of analyzing on different levels is a very useful way of uncovering meaning behind elaboration. While the last Schenker book is not generally available in an English translation, you may consult the books listed in the bibliography by Adele Katz and Felix Salzer, two former students of Schenker, for further details of Schenker's views.

All of these theories were, of course, directed at uncovering the organizational methods used by composers in writing tonal music; finally, a word must be said about twelve-tone serial writing.

In the early 1920s, Arnold Schoenberg suggested that it was possible for a composer to organize a composition upon a different principle than the traditional allegiance to a fixed tonic. He advocated substituting a system of variables in which the twelve tones would be related only to each other rather than to one all-important center. The composition was controlled by a theme, the *Grundgestalt,* which, ideally, contained all of the possible twelve pitches used only once. From this basic germ, one abstracted the *Grundreihe,* the basic set or row of pitches, which was then used for the remainder of the composition. While the pitch order remained unchanged, variation was possible, not only by rhythmic means and the free interchange of octaves, but also by the use of inversion, retrogression, and transposition. Octave doubling was eliminated so as not to emphasize particular tones, and the row was used exclusively for all horizontal (melodic) and vertical (harmonic) activity.

In the collection of essays published under the title *Style and Idea,*[4] Schoenberg left a brief account of this method of composition; a more detailed discussion is available in the English translation by Humphrey Searle of Joseph Rufer's *Composition with Twelve Notes.*

While the discussion here of organizational theories of romantic and modern music has been necessarily brief, the theorists and authors cited are among those that must be studied if the details of contemporary music are to be understood. Such a study in depth of complex music, rather than being the province of an introductory theory course, must be left for the serious study of composition.

[4] Arnold Schoenberg, *Style and Idea* (New York: The Philosophical Library, 1950).

Chapter 16

Solving Figured Bass

Beginning with the concerted style of the early baroque period, circa 1600, composers wrote a *continuo* part to accompany vocal and instrumental melodies. This continuo part supplied the harmonic support for the vocal line in an opera or the instrumental lines in a trio sonata. The part was intended to be played on a keyboard or harmonic instrument, such as the organ, harpsichord, or lute, and supported by a string instrument that played the bass line. This produced what was essentially a *homophonic* texture—an all-important melodic line supported by the less important harmonic background of the continuo. This was a plainer, more direct harmonic style—sometimes called *accompanied monody*—that was very different from the earlier Renaissance texture, which typically, had consisted of an interweaving of several equally important contrapuntal lines.

Along with this harmonic background, composers invented a system of figures to avoid writing out all of the notes that the keyboard instrument actually played. The notation consisted of arabic figures, placed above or below a single bass line, which indicated the intervals in the chords. The player was free to improvise an accompaniment in agreement with these indicated harmonies. You should review the details of this figuration that were given earlier in Chapter 5.

By the eighteenth century, the art of improvising an accompaniment from a figured bass had been raised to a high level, and many contemporary treatises advocated the teaching of harmony by the solution of figured basses. While this book has followed the usual practice of teaching part writing in the open four-part

SATB vocal style, you should also have some experience in solving figured basses in a keyboard style. The keyboard part should be written so that it is playable on the piano, the left hand part consisting of the bass line, the right hand playing the three upper voices within the compass of an octave.

Teaching harmony by the solution of figured basses is another way of separating the problems of part writing and chord choice; the given figures allow no choice of harmony, so one is free to concentrate upon making the voice leading as smooth and interesting as possible. The basic problem for you is the opposite of writing a good bass to a given melody; you must discover an interesting upper part that fits with the given bass. While there are no hard-and-fast rules that guarantee a good solution to a figured bass, the following models will be useful in helping you isolate the basic problems.

MODELS FOR PRACTICE

These models should be played at the keyboard, first in the keys indicated and then transposed to other major and minor keys; the minor keys will normally use the raised leading tone, except in a descending scale. As a rule, in constructing the top melodic part in relation to the given bass, contrary and oblique motion are preferable to similar motion. Observe the ordinary rules for part writing and doubling; avoid diminished and augmented triads in root position, except as part of a sequence. Unacceptable parallel perfect fifths can be inverted to make parallel fourths, which are then usable.

Figure 506

Moving within one chord

Figure 507

Connecting different root position chords
1. Fifth related

2. Second related

3. Third related

(continued)

4. Combinations: Root position chords

(Fifth and second)
(third and second)
(Fifth and fourth)
(Fifth and third)

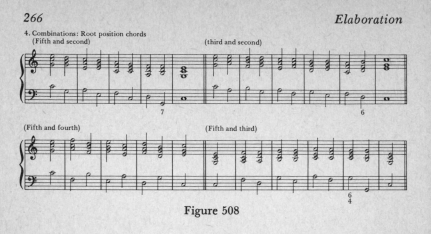

Figure 508

Connecting root position and inversions

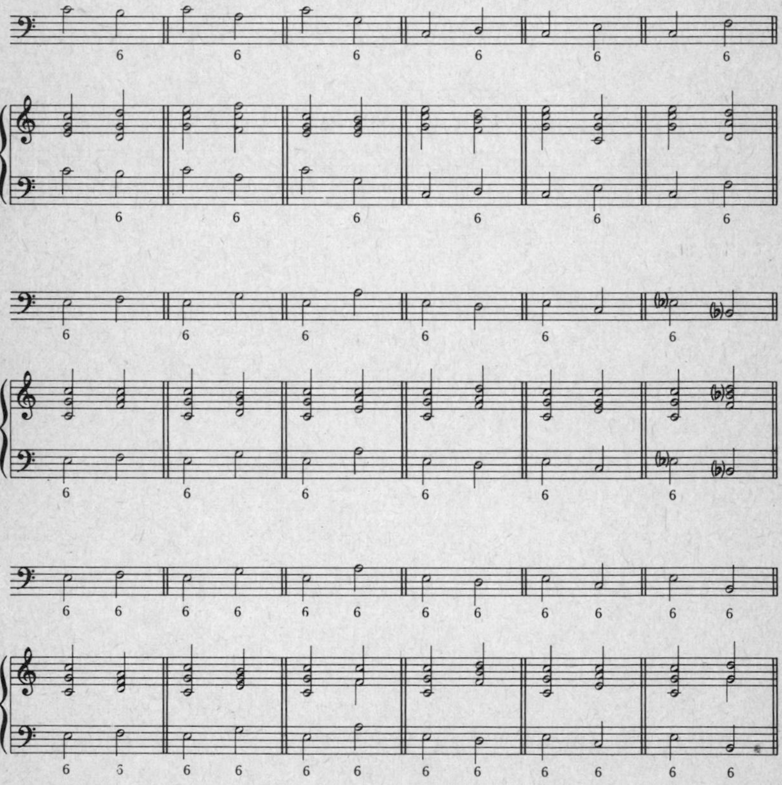

Figure 509

Seventh Chords: Common resolutions

Figure 510

Nonharmonic Tones

(continued)

Figure 511

EXERCISES

Solve the following figured basses in keyboard style (solutions may
also be made in SATB vocal style), paying particular attention to the
melodic character of the topmost part:

1.

2.

3.

4.

5.

Figure 512

Chapter 17

Analysis and Score-Reading

The average performing musician, amateur or professional, is primarily concerned with music written after 1700, and a great part of this practical repertoire is instrumental music that comes from the classic and romantic periods. The average pianist, vocalist, or orchestral instrumentalist is more familiar with the music of Mozart, Haydn, Beethoven, Schubert, Schumann, Brahms, and Debussy than he is with earlier or later music. Most music theory courses, on the other hand, attempt to teach basic harmonic techniques derived from earlier baroque practice; these are usually presented in a four-voice vocal format (SATB).

The student who has learned this kind of classic four-part chorale style, then, often has difficulty in discovering the same principles of voice leading in the instrumental texture of a Mozart or Beethoven piano sonata. The difficulty generally occurs because (1) the instrumental texture is much more elaborate than the chorale style—often consisting of scale passages, arpeggios, nonharmonic decoration, and so on—or (2) the music is often presented in the form of a *score,* which contains other complications, such as different clefs and instrumental transpositions. The purpose of this chapter is to examine the more common instrumental formats and to show the student how to cope with these added complexities in reading and analysis.

KEYBOARD STYLE

The piano writing of the classic period is often a kind of figural elaboration of a simple harmonic background. This keyboard elaboration uses *arpeggios,* or *broken chords, scale passages,* and various kinds of nonharmonic decoration, all being unified

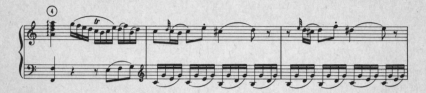

From W. A. Mozart, *Sonatas and Fantasies for the Piano*, edited by Nathan Broder, copyright © 1956 by Theodore Presser Co. Reprinted by permission.

Figure 513a. Mozart, Sonata K. 279

Figure 513b. Reduction

Figure 513a. Sonata (*continued*)

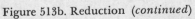

Figure 513b. Reduction (*continued*)

by the recurrence of important thematic motives. One can analyze this music, not only by following the melodic development of the themes, but also by simplifying the texture and discovering the underlying harmonic-tonal progressions.

For example, let us look at the exposition of the first movement of the Piano Sonata no. 1 by Mozart, which is given below. The first sixteen measures give us the principal thematic material and establish the tonic key of C major. The contrasting material ends with a strong cadence in the dominant key of G major at bar 31; the closing material or *coda* extends the exposition to bar 38. Despite the almost constant melodic motion in sixteenth notes throughout the exposition, it is clear that the harmonic changes are moving at a much slower pace. If we think in larger harmonic units of triads and seventh chords we see that each chord may be retained for a half beat, one beat, two beats, or, in many cases, for a whole measure.

In order to see how the principles of four-part harmony are being used here by the composer, we will reduce the elaborate melodic-rhythmic activity and show the basic harmonic changes in four-voice texture. The simplification is made by eliminating broken chords (as in the left-hand part of measure 5), by omitting the passing tones from a scale passage (as in bar 17), and by dropping the neighboring notes, appoggiaturas, and suspensions that are appended to the essential chord tones. The bars are numbered in the reduction to facilitate comparison with the original.

One should play through the original sonata and then the reduction, studying carefully what kinds of decoration Mozart has invented to give life to the music. In many cases the essential impetus is primarily a rhythmic one, the choice of the harmonic background being less important than the motivic activity in the foreground.

▪ Go now to pages 272–273 and 274–275 for the Mozart Sonata.

You should now choose one of the simpler keyboard compositions of Mozart, Haydn, or Beethoven and make a similar harmonic reduction. Begin by eliminating those less essential decorative notes, trying to discover the implied chord that controls the music.

SOLO INSTRUMENT (OR VOICE) WITH ACCOMPANIMENT

This format may contain the same kind of elaborate texture, but it also involves reading from three different staves, which may employ two or three different clefs. Sonatas for violin, flute, or oboe and piano will use an additional treble clef for the solo line.

Figure 514. Piston, Sonatina for Violin and Harpsichord (Piano)

Copyright 1948 by Boosey and Hawkes, Inc. Reprinted by permission.

A composition for cello, bassoon, or trombone and piano will normally use the bass clef for the solo instrument.

Figure 515. Marcello, Sonata opus 1, no. 4

Edited by A. Piatti, copyright 1947 by International Music Company. Reprinted by permission.

A more complex reading problem occurs if the solo instrument utilizes a third clef. This will commonly occur in a sonata for viola and piano, since the viola normally uses the alto clef, or in a sonata for cello, bassoon, or trombone and piano, where the tenor clef is often used for passages in the higher registers.

Figure 516. C. P. E. Bach, Sonata for Viola and Piano

Figured bass realization by Giuseppe Piccioli, edited by William Primrose, copyright 1955 by International Music Company. Reprinted by permission.

Figure 517. Weber, Andante and Hungarian Rondo

Edited by Simon Kovar, copyright © 1956 by International Music Company. Reprinted by permission.

You should review the earlier material on clefs (p. 21) and practice with the alto and tenor clefs so that you have some practical facility in reading these. They are absolutely essential for reading string quartets and orchestral scores.

Students frequently attempt to learn to read the alto clef by thinking of the letter names in relation to those of the treble clef.

Figure 518

This method not only gives the wrong octave, but assures that the student will never become proficient in reading the alto clef. The correct way to acquire facility in clef reading is by establishing a few key reference points and reading in relation to these. For example, in reading a viola part in the alto clef, the three octaves of the note C are key reference points.

Figure 519

Middle C is the center line of the staff; the low C represents the tuning of the lowest string of the viola, and is therefore the lowest note that will occur; notes higher than the c″, if used for an extended period, will usually be written in the treble clef.

The lines of the staff are encompassed by two triads, above and below the middle C.

Figure 520

The spaces can be learned by memorizing the following chords:

Figure 521

With these reference points, and some practice, the reading of viola parts in the alto clef will not be difficult. The same procedure may be applied to the tenor clef.

Figure 522

TRIOS, QUARTETS AND SMALL ENSEMBLES

There are several groupings of string instruments that utilize the clefs just discussed and for which a sizable literature has been developed over the past 250 years. The literature for these small ensembles is often referred to as *chamber music;* the most common groupings are:

String Trio

Figure 523. Beethoven, Trio opus 8

String Quartet

Figure 524. Beethoven, Quartet opus 18, no. 1

String Orchestra (or String Quintet)

Figure 525. Stravinsky, Concerto in D for String Orchestra

Less common groupings include quintets and sextets with double viola or cello parts, or both.

When the piano is included as a member of the chamber music ensemble, this is usually referred to as a *piano trio* (violin, cello, and piano), a *piano quartet* (violin, viola, cello, and piano), or a *piano quintet* (string quartet and piano).

Chamber music ensembles may also include one or more wind instruments, along with string instruments and piano, or may consist entirely of wind instruments as, for example, a *brass quartet* or a *woodwind quintet*. The use of certain wind instruments—for example the clarinet, English horn, trumpet, and French horn—introduces into the score-reading the problem of *transposition* (see Appendix 2).

THE FULL ORCHESTRAL SCORE

When a composer writes a work for *orchestra* (that is, a large ensemble of mixed instruments), he usually prepares a score that shows what instruments are to perform and, at any moment in the composition, exactly what each instrument is expected to do. The score is thus a composite made up of all the individual instrumental parts. It is primarily of use to the conductor, or leader of the orchestra, in rehearsing the ensemble for a performance. Over a period of time, certain conventions have been established for the reading and writing of such a score, and, while these have not always been arrived at by very logical means, they have the force of established custom.

The *symphony orchestra,* of the eighteenth, nineteenth, and early twentieth centuries consists of a large ensemble of woodwind, brass, percussion, and string instruments. The exact makeup of the orchestra, which varies with period and composer, is called the *instrumentation* of the work. This is usually listed on the first page of the score. By custom the groups of instruments are arranged in the score, from top to bottom, in the order given below; the instruments within each group generally being arranged from high (small) to low (large).

Woodwinds	(Piccolo)		Flute
	Flute	*or*	(Piccolo)
	Oboe		
	(English horn)		
	Clarinet		
	(Bass clarinet)		
	Bassoon		
	(Contrabassoon)		

Brass	Trumpet		French horn
	French horn	*or*	Trumpet
	Trombone		
	Tuba		

Percussion	Timpani (Kettle drums)
	Snare drum
	Bass drum
	Cymbals
	Triangle
	Tam-tam
	Tambourine
	Glockenspiel
	Bells

{ Harp
Piano
Celesta
Organ

Strings { First Violin
Second Violin
Viola
Cello
String Bass

Not all of these instruments will occur in every score; a sample first page of a typical work for large orchestra is given on page 284.

The chart on page 285 shows the actual instrumentation of the most popular symphonies in the literature from Mozart to Mahler.

The reading of a score, either of a chamber music or orchestral work, should be practiced systematically, not only silently but also at the piano. To gain any proficiency you will have to invent progressively more difficult problems, starting with clef reading and going on to the more complex transposition. (At the end of the text there are appendixes that give the foreign names for the orchestral instruments, with their ranges and transpositions.)

In the early years of the twentieth century, it became apparent to some composers that the increasing complexity of modern music eventually would necessitate the writing of all scores at *concert pitch,* that is, without transpositions. Prokofiev and Schoenberg, to mention two who advocated this, both wrote their mature orchestral scores at the actual sounding pitches, regardless of the instruments employed. This is a sound practice which has generally been followed by many recent composers; the perception of a new, complex, and dissonant work, particularly an atonal or serial composition, is greatly simplified by this procedure. Of course, when the individual orchestral parts are

Figure 526. Strauss, *Don Juan*

INSTRUMENTATION OF THIRTY POPULAR SYMPHONIES (1788–1896)

Instrument	Mozart No.40 (G minor) 1788	Mozart No.41 (Jupiter) 1788	Haydn No.100 (Military) 1794	Haydn No.101 (Clock) 1794	Haydn No.104 (London) 1795	Beethoven No.1 1799	Beethoven No.2 1802	Beethoven No.3 (Eroica) 1803	Beethoven No.4 1806	Beethoven No.5 1807	Beethoven No.6 (Pastorale) 1808	Beethoven No.7 1812	Beethoven No.8 1812	Beethoven No.9 1824	Schubert No.8 (Unfinished) 1822	Schubert No.7 (C major) 1828	Berlioz Sym. Fantastique 1830	Mendelssohn No.4 (Italian) 1833	Schumann No.1 (Spring) 1841	Brahms No.1 1876	Brahms No.2 1877	Brahms No.3 1883	Brahms No.4 1885	Bruckner No.7 1883	Franck D minor 1888	Tchaikovsky No.4 1877	Tchaikovsky No.5 1888	Tchaikovsky No.6 (Pathétique) 1893	Chausson Sym. in B♭ 1890	Mahler No.3 1896
Piccolo			1							1	1			1			(1)						1			1	1 (1)	(1)		1 (2)
Flute	1	1	2	2	2	2	2	2	2	2	2	2	2	2	2	2	2	2	2	2	2	2	2	2	2	2	3	3	3	4
Oboe	2	2	2	2	2	2	2	2	2	2	2	2	2	2	2	2	2	2	2	2	2	2	2	2	2	2	2	2	2	4
English horn																	(1)								1					2
E♭ clarinet																	(1)													2
B♭, A, or C Clar.	2		2	2	2	2	2	2	2	2	2	2	2	2	2	2	2	2	2	2	2	2	2	2	2	2	2	2	2	3
Bass clarinet																									1			1	1	(1)
Bassoon	2	2	2	2	2	2	2	2	2	2	2	2	2	2	2	2	4	2	2	2	2	2	2	2	2	2	2	2	3	4
Contra bassoon										1				1						1		1	1							(1)
Horn	2	2	2	2	2	2	2	3	2	2	2	2	2	4	2	2	4	2	2	4	4	4	4	4	4	4	4	4	4	8
Trumpet		2	2	2	2	2	2	2	2	2	2	2	2	2	2	2	2	2	2	2	2	2	2	3	2	2	2	2	4	4
Cornet à pistons																	2								2					
Trombone										3	2			3	3	3	3		3	3	3	3	3	3	3	3	3	3	3	4
Tuba																	2							Wagnerian 2 Tenor / 2 Bass Tubas				1		1
Timpani		2	2	2	2	2	2	2	2	2	2	2	2	2	2	2	4 (2 players)	2	2	2	2	2	2	3	3	3	3	3	3	2 (2 players)
Snare drum																										✓				✓
Bass drum			✓														✓									✓				✓
Cymbals			✓														✓									✓				✓
Triangle			✓																				✓			✓				✓
Tam-tam																												✓		✓
Tambourine																														
Glockenspiel																														
Bells																														4
Harp																	2												2	2
Strings	✓	✓	✓	✓	✓	✓	✓	✓	✓	✓	✓	✓	✓	✓	✓	✓	✓	✓	✓	✓	✓	✓	✓	✓	✓	✓	✓	✓	✓	✓

Mahler No. 3: { 2 choruses, Alto Solo }

copied from such a concert-pitch score, they must each be
properly transposed for the different instruments. This is a practice that is strongly recommended to all young composers, and,
for clarification, a note should appear at the beginning of the
score to the effect that all instruments are written at their
sounding pitches.

THE ANALYSIS OF AN EXTENDED WORK

The process of music analysis implies the careful examination
of a composition, a detailed study of its component parts, and
its overall characteristics. The aim of such an examination is to
discover what is most effective in the composition and how this
was achieved by the composer. The analysis of works of master
composers by the student serves primarily to acquaint him with
the acceptable conventions of the art in different periods. The
analysis we have done in this text generally has been an examination of short fragments of music to illustrate some small detail.
After such detailed analyses, some overview of the larger aspects
of the work should be attempted. The latter is a somewhat different process when the composition is an extended work like a
movement of a sonata or a symphony.

The overview of a long work is generally concerned with two
areas of investigation: (1) the thematic-melodic form and (2)
the harmonic-tonal design, that is, one traces what happens to
the subject of the work as it progresses through its modulatory
journey. It is still necessary to begin by looking at the details of
the work in order to assemble enough evidence upon which to
make larger judgments. Heinrich Schenker used the terms foreground, middle ground, and background to characterize this
process of working from the level of detail to that of the larger
picture. At each change of level one suppresses the least essential
details of the old level, in order to retain what is most essential
for the new level.

There is generally good agreement among theorists as to how
one symbolizes the analysis of harmonic details in a composition;
there is less general agreement as to how to symbolize its larger
thematic-formal aspects. This latter is usually shown in words or
diagrams, or a combination of these and staff notation. Schenker
worked out a technique, based upon a series of graphs, that

charted in music notation the different levels of an analysis, but this technique is too succinct and specialized for the beginning theory student. For the present, it will be sufficient to diagram the thematic and tonal developments of a work in a manner similar to the following illustration which examines the third movement of the Symphony no. 3 by Johannes Brahms. You should obtain a score and a recording of this work and listen to it several times.

It is clear from the first hearing that this composition presents its main theme several times and intersperses these occurrences with other contrasting material. The idea of a recurring idea suggests that the overall form will be a rondo (see Appendix 4 for diagrams of forms).

The principal theme, twelve measures long, is an eight-measure period with a four-measure extension in the key of C minor. The first phrase, played by the cellos, is:

Figure 527

This is followed by a repetition of the same twelve-measure period played an octave higher by the first violins. The next sixteen measures present a contrasting theme beginning in C major and modulating to A minor

Figure 528

The first theme then returns, in three octaves, played by horn, oboe, and flute. So far the thematic design may be symbolized:

a   a   b   a

This might also be symbolized:

At this point there is a double bar and a new key signature—that of A flat major—denoting a new large part or section. This begins with an eight-measure period; the first phrase, played by the woodwinds, is:

Figure 529

As in the first large part, this eight-measure theme is repeated, and is then followed by another, contrasting eight-measure period, played by the strings in the distant key of E major.

Figure 530

After modulating at the end of the second four-measure phrase, this section is followed by a return to the first theme of this part in A flat major. A twelve-measure transition leads back to the first part in the main key of C minor. The second large part has the same form as did part one:

‖: c:‖   d   c   Transition

Figure 531

The entire part one then recurs substantially as before, and the movement ends with a short coda of thirteen measures.

Before graphing the entire movement, the key structure needs some additional explanation. In part 2, if the key of E major is thought of enharmonically as F flat major, it is more easily related to A flat major (as ♭ VI), the principal key of this part. This is somewhat balanced by the change from C minor to A minor in part 1.

Figure 532

To understand the significance of the main keys of C minor and A flat major, one must look at the key scheme for the other movements of the Symphony no. 3.

First movement:	F major
Second movement:	C major
Third movement:	C minor
Fourth movement:	F minor

It is clear that the C and A flat of the third movement are members of the tonic F minor triad.

As the following schematic design shows, this movement is in the form of a First Rondo. The different themes are symbolized by small letters, with their keys shown below, and the number of measures in each section given above. The larger divisions are symbolized by capital letters.

THIRD MOVEMENT: C MINOR
FIRST RONDO FORM (*ABA*)

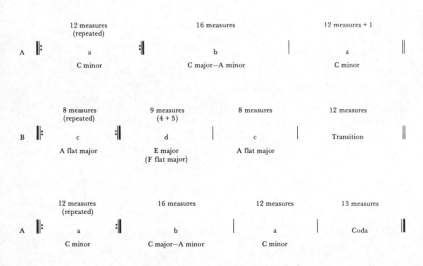

Figure 533. Brahms, Symphony no. 3

Appendix 1

Foreign-Language Names
for Orchestral Instruments

In the early nineteenth century composers of many countries accepted the convention that the names of instruments, and the directions written in a score, would be in Italian. This language was almost universally used to indicate the tempo, dynamics, and other directions to the performers. However, the more nationalistic movements that took place in the latter half of the nineteenth century seemed to encourage the use of programmatic titles, and directions to the players, as well as the names of instruments, in the vernacular language of the composer. Below are the names and the common abbreviations of the orchestral instruments in English, Italian, French, and German.

INSTRUMENT NAMES AND ABBREVIATIONS

Woodwind Instruments

English	Italian	French	German
Piccolo (Picc.)	Flauto piccolo (Fl. picc.)	Petite flute (Pte. fl.)	Kleine Flöte (Kl. Fl.)
Flute (Fl.)	Flauto (Fl.)	Flute (Fl.)	Grosse Flöte (Gr. Fl.)

English	*Italian*	*French*	*German*
Oboe (Ob.)	Oboe (Ob.)	Hautbois (Hb.)	Hoboe (Hb.)
English horn (E.H.)	Corno inglese (C. ingl.)	Cor Anglais (Cor. A.)	Englisches Horn (E.H.)
Clarinet (Cl.)	Clarinetto (Cl.)	Clarinette (Cl.)	Klarinette (Kl.)
Bass clarinet (B. Cl.)	Clarinetto basso (Cl. b.)	Clarinette basse (Cl. bs.)	Bassklarinette (Bkl.)
Bassoon (Bssn.)	Fagotto (Fag.)	Basson (Bssn.)	Fagot (Fag.)
Contrabassoon (C. Bssn.)	Contrafagotto (Cfg.)	Contrebasson (C. bssn.)	Kontrafagot (Kfg.)

Brass Instruments

French horn (Hr.)	Corno (Cor.)	Cor (Cor.)	Horn (Hr.)
Trumpet (Trp.)	Tromba (Tr.)	Trompette (Tr.)	Trompete (Tr.)
Trombone (Trb.)	Trombone (Trb.)	Trombone (Tromb.)	Posaune (Pos.)
Tuba (Tb.)	Tuba (Tb.)	Tuba (Tb.)	Tuba (Tb.)

Percussion Instruments

Timpani (Timp.) or Kettle drums (K.D.)	Timpani (Timp.)	Timbales (Timb.)	Pauken (Pk.)
Snare drum (S.D.)	Tamburo militare (Tamb. milit.)	Tambour militaire (Tamb. milit.)	Kleine Trommel (Kl. Tr.)
Bass drum (B.D.)	Gran Cassa (Gr. Cassa)	Grosse caisse (Gr. c.)	Grosse Trommel (Gr. Tr.)

English	Italian	French	German
Cymbals (Cym.)	Piatti (Piat.)	Cymbales (Cymb.)	Becken (Beck.)
Triangle (Trgl.)	Triangolo (Trgl.)	Triangle (Trg.)	Triangel (Trgl.)
Tam-tam (T.-t.) or Gong	Tam-Tam (T.-T.)	Tam-tam (T.-t.)	Tam-tam (T.-t.)
Tambourine (Tamb.)	Tambourino (Tamb.)	Tambour de Basque (T. de B.)	Tamburin (Tamb.)
Glockenspiel (Glock.)	Campanelli (Cmplli.)	Carrillon (Car.)	Glockenspiel (Glsp.)
Chimes (Bells)	Campane (Camp.)	Cloches (Cloch.)	Glocken (Glock.)

String Instruments

English	Italian	French	German
Violin (Vln.)	Violino (Vln.)	Violon (Vl.)	Violine (Vl.)
Viola (Vla.)	Viola (Va.)	Alto (A.)	Bratsche (Br.)
Cello (C.) or (Vc.)	Violoncello (Vlc.)	Violoncelle (Vc.)	Violoncell (Vc.)
Double Bass (D. Bs.)	Contrabasso (Cb.)	Contre basse (C.b.)	Kontrabass (Kb.)

Other Instruments

English	Italian	French	German
Harp (Hp.)	Arpa (Arp.)	Harpe (Hp.)	Harfe (Har.)
Piano	Pianoforte (P.-f.)	Piano	Klavier (Klav.)
Harpsichord	Clavicembalo (Cembalo)	Clavecin	Kielflugel
Organ (Org.)	Organo	Orgue	Orgel

Appendix 2

Range and Transposition
of Orchestral Instruments

Natural horns and trumpets were most commonly found in the following sizes, sounding as indicated:

Natural horns in:

B flat (alto) sounded a major second lower

A sounded a minor third lower

G sounded a perfect fourth lower

F sounded a perfect fifth lower

E sounded a minor sixth lower

E flat sounded a major sixth lower

D sounded a minor seventh lower

C sounded a perfect octave lower

B flat (basso) sounded a major ninth lower

Natural trumpets in:

F sounded a perfect fourth higher

E sounded a major third higher

E flat sounded a minor third higher

D sounded a major second higher

C sounded as written

B flat sounded a major second lower

A sounded a minor third lower

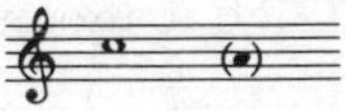

MODERN ORCHESTRAL INSTRUMENTS

Instrument	Written Range	Sound Production	Transposition
Piccolo		Air column across edge of tube	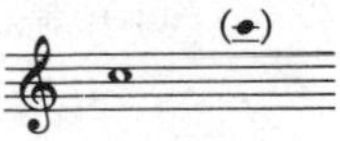
Flute		Air column across edge of tube	
Oboe	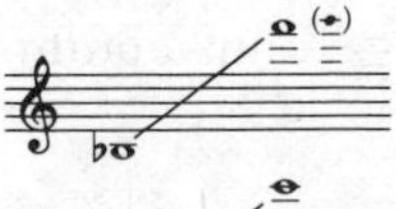	Double reed	
English horn (F)	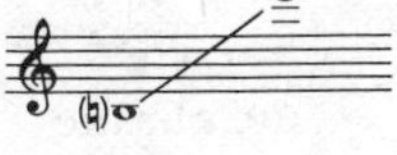	Double reed	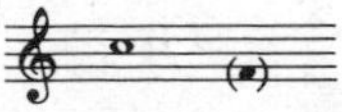

Instrument	Written Range	Sound Production	Transposition

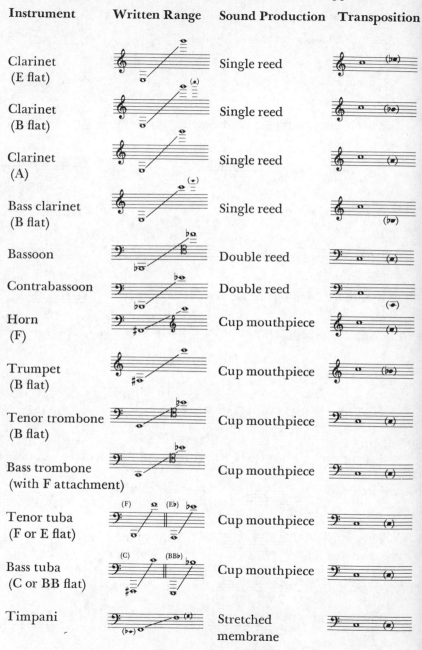

Clarinet (E flat)	Single reed
Clarinet (B flat)	Single reed
Clarinet (A)	Single reed
Bass clarinet (B flat)	Single reed
Bassoon	Double reed
Contrabassoon	Double reed
Horn (F)	Cup mouthpiece
Trumpet (B flat)	Cup mouthpiece
Tenor trombone (B flat)	Cup mouthpiece
Bass trombone (with F attachment)	Cup mouthpiece
Tenor tuba (F or E flat)	Cup mouthpiece
Bass tuba (C or BB flat)	Cup mouthpiece
Timpani	Stretched membrane

Instrument	Written Range	Sound Production	Transposition

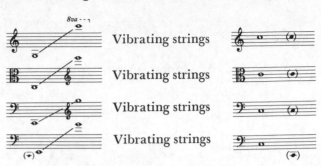

Violin   Vibrating strings

Viola   Vibrating strings

Cello   Vibrating strings

String bass   Vibrating strings

Figure 534

Appendix 3

Diagrams of Homophonic Forms

SMALL FORMS

Phrase

Final Cadence

Period

Phrase 1	Phrase 2
Non-final Cadence	Final Cadence

Phrase Group

Phrase 1	Phrase 2	Phrase 3
Non-final	Non-final	Final

Double Period

Period I		Period II	
Phrase 1	Phrase 2	Phrase 3	Phrase 4
Non-final	Semi-final	Non-final	Final

PART FORMS

Two-Part Form (Binary)

Part I - A	Part II - B (or A')
Period (or Double Period)	Period (or Double Period)
Tonic Dominant	Dominant Tonic

Three-Part Form (Ternary)

Part I - A	Part II - B	Part III - A'
Period (or Double Period)	Period (or Double Period)	Period (or Double Period)
Tonic	Dominant (or Relative Major)	Tonic

Two-Part Form with Trio

A	B	A
Menuetto (Two-Part)	Trio (Two-Part)	Da Capo (of Menuetto)
a b	c d	a b

Three-Part Form with Trio

A	B	A
Scherzo (Three-Part)	Trio (Three-Part)	Da Capo (Scherzo)
a b a	c d c	a b a

LARGE FORMS

Rondo Forms

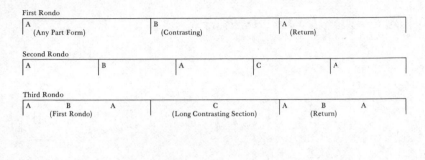

First Rondo

A	B	A
(Any Part Form)	(Contrasting)	(Return)

Second Rondo

A	B	A	C	A

Third Rondo

A B A	C	A B A
(First Rondo)	(Long Contrasting Section)	(Return)

Sonatina Form

	Exposition		Transition		Recapitulation	
1st Theme		2nd Theme		1st Theme		2nd Theme
Tonic		Dominant (Relative Major)		Tonic		Tonic

Sonata Form

	Exposition			Development	Recapitulation			
Intro.	1st Theme	2nd Theme	Closing Theme	Fragments of Themes-Modulatory	1st Th.	2nd Th.	Cl. Th.	Coda
	Tonic	Dominant ———— (Relative Major ————)			Tonic	Tonic	Tonic	

Appendix 4

Bach Chorales for Analysis

Figure 535. Chorale no. 184, "Christ lag in Todesbanden"

Figure 536. Chorale no. 263, "Jesu, meine Freude"

Figure 537. Chorale no. 195, "Wie schön leuchtet der Morgenstern"

Figure 538. Chorale no. 179, "Wachet auf, ruft uns die Stimme"

(continued)

Figure 539. Chorale no. 306, "O Mensch, bewein' dein'Sünde gross"

(continued)

Figure 540. Chorale no. 107, "Herzlich lieb hab' ich dich, o Herr"

Bibliography

BOOKS ON MUSIC THEORY

Boatwright, Howard. *Introduction to the Theory of Music.* New York: W. W. Norton, 1956.

Dallin, Leon. *Foundations in Music Theory.* Belmont, Calif.: Wardsworth, 1967.

Forte, Allen. *Tonal Harmony in Concept and Practice.* New York: Holt, Rinehart and Winston, 1962.

Goetschius, Percy. *Material Used in Musical Composition.* New York: G. Schirmer, 1895.

Hindemith, Paul. *Traditional Harmony.* Book I. New York: Associated Music Publishers, 1944.

Kohs, Ellis B. *Music Theory.* 2 vols. New York: Oxford University Press, 1961.

McHose, Allen Irvine. *Basic Principles of the Technique of 18th and 19th Century Composition.* New York: Appleton-Century-Crofts, 1951.

————. *The Contrapuntal Harmonic Technique of the 18th Century.* New York: Appleton-Century-Crofts, 1947.

Ottman, Robert W. *Advanced Harmony.* Englewood Cliffs, N.J.: Prentice-Hall, 1961.

————. *Elementary Harmony.* Englewood Cliffs, New Jersey: Prentice-Hall, 1961.

Piston, Walter. *Harmony.* New York: W. W. Norton, 1962.

Sessions, Roger. *Harmonic Practice.* New York: Harcourt, Brace and World, 1951.

Tischler, Hans. *Practical Harmony.* Boston: Allyn and Bacon, 1964.

Wedge, George A. *Applied Harmony.* New York: G. Schirmer, Book I, 1930, Book II, 1931.

BOOKS ON ORCHESTRATION, COUNTERPOINT AND FORM

Forsyth, Cecil. *Orchestration.* 2nd edition. New York: Macmillan, 1935.

Goetschius, Percy. *Applied Counterpoint.* 5th edition. New York: G. Schirmer, 1915.

————. *The Homophonic Forms of Musical Composition.* New York: G. Schirmer, 1898.

————. *The Larger Forms of Musical Composition.* New York: G. Schirmer, 1915.

Hindemith, Paul. *The Craft of Musical Composition.* Vol. I. New York: Associated Music Publishers, 1945.

Jeppesen, Knud. *Counterpoint.* Translated by Glen Haydon. Englewood Cliffs, N.J.: Prentice Hall, 1939.

Jones, George Thaddeus. *Music Composition.* Evanston, Illinois: Summy-Birchard, 1963.

Katz, Adele. *Challenge to Musical Tradition.* London: Putnam, 1947.

Kennan, Kent. *Counterpoint Based on Eighteenth Century Practice.* Englewood Cliffs, N.J.: Prentice-Hall, 1959.

————. *The Technique of Orchestration.* Englewood Cliffs, New Jersey: Prentice-Hall, 1952.

Read, Gardner. *Thesaurus of Orchestral Devices.* New York: Pitman, 1953.

Reti, Rudolph. *The Thematic Process in Music.* New York: Macmillan, 1951.

————. *Tonality, Atonality, Pantonality.* London: Rockliff, 1958.

Rogers, Bernard. *The Art of Orchestration.* New York: Appleton-Century-Crofts, 1951.

Rufer, Josef. *Composition with Twelve Notes.* Translated by Humphrey Searle. New York: Macmillan, 1954.

Salzer, Felix. *Structural Hearing.* 2 vols. New York: C. Boni, 1952.

Schoenberg, Arnold. *Style and Idea.* New York: Philosophical Library, 1950.

Soderlund, Gustave Fredric. *Direct Approach to Counterpoint.* New York: Appleton-Century-Crofts, 1947.

Stravinsky, Igor. *Poetics of Music.* Translated by Arthur Knodel and Ingolf Dahl. Cambridge, Massachusetts: Harvard University Press, 1947.

Abbreviations, 78
Accents, 77
Accidentals, 23
Acoustics, 3
Alla breve, 19
Amplitude, 3
Anacrusis, 27, 104
Analysis, 271
    of an extended work, 286
Anticipation, 171, 183
Appoggiatura, 171, 186
Arabic numerals, 61
Articulation, 76
Artificial division, 19

Bar line, 15, 26
    double, 26
Bass line, 151
Beat, 14
Bitonality, 57
Brass, 282

Cadence, 86
    authentic (full) , perfect, 106,
        143, 150
    authentic (full) , imperfect,
        107, 143
    clausula vera, 87
    deceptive, 108, 151
    feminine, 104
    final, 106, 143
    half, 108, 143, 151
    harmonic, 143
    interior, 108, 143

    masculine, 104
    melodic, 106, 150
    Phrygian, 92
    plagal, imperfect, 143
Cambiata, 189
Chamber music, 281
Chorales, Bach, for analysis, 300
Chord, 49
    added tone, 57
    altered, 97, 229
    appoggiatura, 247
    augmented sixth, 237
    choice, 141
    common, 94
    connection (principles of) , 123
    connection summary, 134
    dominant, altered, 241
    eleventh, 54, 220
    mystic, 55
    Neapolitan, 234
    ninth, 54, 215
    pivot, 94
    seventh, 53, 54, 199
    thirteenth, 54, 222
Chromatic third relation, 251
Chromaticism, 229
Circle of fifths, 35
Clef, 21
    alto, 21, 278
    bass (F) , 21
    movable (C) , 21
    tenor, 21, 279
    treble (G) , 21
Coda, 26

Codetta, 110
Comma
    Pythagorean, 45
    syntonic, 47
Compound time, 18
Concert pitch, 283
Conical, 7
Consonance, 49, 120
Continuo, 61, 263
Cross relation (false) , 130
Cylindrical, 7

Da capo (D.C.) , 26
Dal segno (D.S.) , 26
Dashes, 77
Dissonance, 49, 51, 120
Dominant, 60
    altered, 241
    secondary, 231
Dots, 13, 77
Doubling, voice, 114
Duplet, 19
Duration, 3
Dynamics, 75
    terms for, 74

Enharmonic, 24
Ensemble, 280
Equal temperament, 10, 47
Escape tone, 172, 188
Expression marks, 73
Extension (melody writing) , 110

Figured bass, 61, 263
Finalis, 85
Flat, 23
    double, 24
Forms
    homophonic, 298
    large, 299
    part, 298
    rondo, 289, 299
    small, 298
    sonata, 299
    sonatina, 299
    strophic, 102
Four-part writing, 113
Fourth, augmented, 119
Free tone, 172, 192
Frequency, 3
Fundamental, 5, 85
Fundamental bass, 87

Grundgestalt, 261
Grundreihe, 261

Half step, 10, 31
Harmonic alteration, 243

Instrumentation, 282, 285
Instruments
    names of, 291
    range of, 294
    transposition, 294
Intensity, 3
Interval, 31, 36
    compound, 30, 40
    harmonic, 31
    inversion, 39
    melodic, 31
    simple, 39, 40
Inversions
    first, 53, 202
    second, 51, 53, 203
    third, 203

Key feeling, 91
Keynote, 32
Keys
    closely related, 40
    foreign names for, 81
    major, 32, 65
    minor, 33, 65
    parallel, 40
    relative major, 40
    relative minor, 40
    signature, 34

Landini sixth, 188
Leading tone, 60, 86, 119
Ledger lines, 22
Ligature, 12
Loop, 4

Measure, 15
Mediant, 60
Melodic alteration, 230
Melody
    analysis, 159
    harmonization, 159
    writing, 101
Meter, 14
Metronomic notation, 16

Mode, 42
    Aeolian, 42
    Church, 42
    Dorian, 42
    Ionian, 42
    Locrian, 42
    Lydian, 42
    Mixolydian, 42
    Phrygian, 42
Modulation, 94
    chain, 251
    change of mode, 249
    chromatic, 95
    common chord, 94
    common tone, 252
    direct, 96
    remote, 249
Motion, 116
    conjunct, 101, 152
    contrary, 116
    disjunct, 101
    oblique, 116
    similar, 116
Motive (Motif), 102
Musica falsa, 230
Musica ficta, 86, 91, 98, 230

Natural (sign), 23
Neighboring tone, 171, 176
Neapolitan, 6, 234
Node, 4
Noise, 3
Nonharmonic tones (nonchord), 169
Notation, 11
Note values, 11

Octave, 10
    designations, 25
    equivalence, 10
Orchestra
    score, 281
    string, 281
    symphony, 282
Overtones, 5
Overtone series, 5

Part writing, principals of, 124
Partial, 5
Passing tone, 171, 172
Pedal, 172, 190
Percussion, 282
Period, 102
    double, 102

Phrase, 102
    antecedent, 104
    consequent, 104
    group, 102
    member, 102
Phrasing, 76
Picardy third (*tierce de Picardie*),
    52, 92
"pick-up" note, 27
Pipe, closed, 8
    open, 7
Prohibitions, in four-part writing,
    118

Quartet
    brass, 281
    piano, 281
    string, 280
Quintet
    piano, 281
    string, 281
    woodwind, 281

Ranges (voice), 114
    alto, 114
    bass, 114
    soprano, 114
    tenor, 114
Relative major, 40
Relative minor, 40
Rests, 11
Roman numerals, 63
Root, 50, 85
Root movement, 89
Root movement chart, 149
Rhythm, 11

Scale, 31
    chromatic, 24, 32
    degrees, 60
    degrees, foreign names, 80
    diatonic, 23
    harmonic minor, 33
    major, 32
    major-minor, 93
    melodic minor, 33
    minor, 33
    natural minor, 33
    pentatonic, 44
    synthetic, 44
    tempered, 5
    twelve-tone, 258
    whole tone, 43

Score reading, 271
Second
    augmented, 33, 119
    major, 32
    minor, 32
Secondary dominant, 97, 231
Serial (series, twelve-tone), 261
Series, overtone, 5
Sharp, 23
    double, 24
Simple time, 18
Slurs, 77
Solfege syllables, 22
Solo instrument, accompanied, 277
Staff, 20
Strings, 283
Style
    keyboard, 271
    terms for, 75
Subdominant, 60
Submediant, 60
Subtonic, 60
Suspension, 171, 179
Symbolization, 59
Syncopation, 20

Temperament, 45
    equal, 10, 47
    mean tone, 47
Tempo, 16
    terms for, 73
Terms
    dynamic, 74
    foreign language, 73
    style, 75
    tempo, 73
Ties, 13
Timbre, 3, 6
Time
    artificial division, 19

common, 19
compound, 18
signature, 17
simple, 18
Tonality, 85
Tone cluster, 56
Tonic, 60, 85
Tremolo, 80
Triads
    augmented, 53, 232
    diminished, 53
    first inversion, 53, 131
    fifth apart, 126
    major, 53
    minor, 53
    repeated, 125
    root position, 52, 53
    second apart, 127
    second inversion, 51, 53, 132
    third apart, 129
Trio
    piano, 281
    string, 280
Triplet, 19
Tritone, 50
Tritone sonority, 245
Tuning system, 10, 45
    just intonation, 46
    Pythagorean, 45

Vibrating air column, 6
Vibrating bars, 9
Vibrating strings, 4
Vibrations, 3
Volume, 3

Wave, sound, 3
Wedges, 78
Whole step, 31
Woodwinds, 282